Key Themes in Policing

Series editors: **Megan O'Neill**, University of Dundee,
Marisa Silvestri, University of Kent and
Stephen Tong, Kingston University

The Key Themes in Policing series is designed to fill a growing need for titles which reflect the importance of incorporating 'research informed policing' and engaging with evidence-based policing within Higher Education curricula.

Also available

Practical Psychology for Policing
By **Jason Roach**

Challenges in Mental Health and Policing
By **Ian Cummins**

Towards Ethical Policing
By **Dominic Wood**

Critical Perspectives on Police Leadership
By **Claire Davis** and **Marisa Silvestri**

Police Occupational Culture
By **Tom Cockroft**

Policing the Police
By **Michael Rowe**

Miscarriages of Justice
By **Sam Poyser, Angus Nurse** and **Rebecca Milne**

Key Challenges in Criminal Investigation
By **Martin O'Neill**

Plural Policing
By **Colin Rogers**

Understanding Police Intelligence Work
By **Adrian James**

Coming soon

Investigating and Policing Rape
By **Emma Williams**

Editorial advisory board

Find out more at
policy.bristoluniversitypress.co.uk/key-themes-in-policing

NEIGHBOURHOOD POLICING
Context, Practices and Challenges

Carina O'Reilly

P

First published in Great Britain in 2024 by

Policy Press, an imprint of
Bristol University Press
University of Bristol
1–9 Old Park Hill
Bristol
BS2 8BB
UK
t: +44 (0)117 374 6645
e: bup-info@bristol.ac.uk

Details of international sales and distribution partners are available at
policy.bristoluniversitypress.co.uk

© Bristol University Press 2024

British Library Cataloguing in Publication Data
A catalogue record for this book is available from the British Library

ISBN 978-1-4473-6809-0 hardcover
ISBN 978-1-4473-6810-6 paperback
ISBN 978-1-4473-6811-3 ePub
ISBN 978-1-4473-6812-0 ePdf

Cover design: Andrew Corbett
Front cover image: Alamy/Stephen Barnes/Law and Order

Dedicated to Bill Tupman, my mentor and friend, and
Margaret Fenton, always loved and missed.

Contents

Series editor preface

The *Key Themes in Policing Series* aims to provide relevant and useful books to support the growing number of policing modules on both undergraduate and postgraduate programmes. The series also aims to support all those interested in policing from criminology, law, and policing students and policing professionals to those who wish to join policing services. It seeks to respond to the call for research in relevant and under-researched areas in policing encouraged by organisations such as the College of Policing in England and Wales. By producing a range of high-quality, research-informed texts on important areas in policing, contributions to the series support and inform both professional and academic policing curriculums.

We are delighted to welcome *Neighbourhood Policing: Context, Practices and Challenges* by Carina O'Reilly to the *Key Themes in Policing Series*. This book comes at an important moment for policing in several areas of the globe. The early 21st century has already brought many challenges to the legitimacy and practice of policing, from events such as the movement to defund the police to the effects of the COVID-19 pandemic. Questions are being asked about what we want the police to do and how best this should be achieved. Community policing, and the UK version 'Neighbourhood Policing', is often cited as a possible solution to rebuilding trust between the police and the communities they serve. In this book, O'Reilly charts the effects of these events and the wider changing political landscape on the practice of neighbourhood policing. She notes how the original goals of the practice have been reframed, considers how the practice can operate now, especially in a context of reduced funding, and looks to the future of this much-loved but often ill-understood 'bedrock' of policing in the Global North. Specific elements of neighbourhood policing are considered in detail, including visibility, community engagement, problem-solving and partnerships. This text will be essential reading for both researchers and practitioners alike.

About the author

Carina O'Reilly is Senior Lecturer in Criminology at the University of Lincoln. Carina completed her PhD at Anglia Ruskin University with a thesis on neighbourhood policing. She was also previously a local councillor and was Deputy Leader of Cambridge City Council. Carina's current research interests lie in neighbourhood policing and community engagement, and the way this contributes to police confidence and legitimacy, as well as the overlap between politics and policing. She is academic editor of *Policing Insight*, where she contributes regular articles under the series heading 'The Police Student'.

Publications

O'Reilly, C. 2023. Doing the right thing? Value conflicts and community policing. *Policing and Society*, 33(1): 1–17. ISSN 1043-9463.

O'Reilly, C., Agnew-Pauley, W. and Lundrigan, S. 2022. Restoring public confidence through the delivery of improved community policing in Rackhamshire. *Safer Communities*. ISSN 1757-8043.

1

Overview

Introduction

British policing appears to be facing successive legitimacy crises. However, this experience is not confined to the UK. At least since the 1970s, police forces in the Global North seem to have undergone a relentless decline of legitimacy, expressed in a series of confrontations and convulsions. Indeed, the breakdown in the US of the relationship between police and the communities they serve has notoriously been such that some have called for the police to be defunded and replaced.

Some ascribe this loss of legitimacy to neoliberalism and patterns of globalisation, leading to the disincorporation of the working classes through high unemployment and social exclusion (Reiner, 2010). These are a result of economic changes far beyond the control of the police. The outcome has been a gradual disconnection of the police from communities they once served; as well as profound changes to those communities themselves, in a context of increasing democratisation and higher expectations of the police, particularly among marginalised groups.

Community policing has been one response to this rolling crisis. Intended as a way of reconnecting police with communities, it has developed in different shapes in different jurisdictions, and its definition is subsequently ambiguous. Neighbourhood policing is the UK version of community policing, originally rolled out in a three-year project from 2005 to 2008. Neighbourhood policing as a model has become institutionalised in British policing, though in recent years it has come under considerable pressure.

This book provides a critical analysis of neighbourhood policing: charting its peculiarly British roots; the mechanisms by which it was intended to support public confidence in policing; the evidence as to what activities work to do so; and the challenges, both to pursuing those activities and to confidence as a goal in itself. While community policing is a model that has been adopted in many different jurisdictions, this book is focused on the UK, to allow an in-depth understanding of a model that has been described as the 'cornerstone' of the unarmed model of British 'policing by consent' (HMIC, 2017).

This introductory chapter defines community policing and demonstrates how the UK model of neighbourhood policing is differentiated. Community policing is contextualised in global processes of technological development and professionalisation, before the chapter explores why it has been adopted so broadly by so many different places – what is the common problem with policing that community policing hopes to solve? Early examples of community policing are explored; such as the iconic Chicago Alternative Policing Strategy (CAPS) programme. This international context allows us to identify both the commonalities across different examples of community policing, and the particular shape and flavour of the British variety.

One particular commonality is the controversies that arise around it and the resistance to its implementation. Contemporary global issues challenge both communities and their policing, ranging from the difficulties in establishing community policing models in the Global South and post-conflict environments, to current challenges to legitimacy within developed states such as campaigns to defund the police. Such challenges speak to the themes that underpin this book: the importance of the political landscape to the development and support of policing strategies; the inherent tension between the contradictory purposes of policing, as the coercive arm of the state on the one hand, and a service that depends on legitimacy for its effectiveness on the other; and the way confidence and legitimacy – particularly within the British model of policing by consent – depends on connections and relationships: the affective over the effective.

This book is aimed at academics, students, police officers and anybody with a practical interest in how to effectively undertake neighbourhood policing. It will show how, and perhaps more importantly why, the mechanisms of neighbourhood policing support public confidence in policing, and how to implement these effectively in the context of changing demand and limited resources.

Context

Community policing has often been described as more of a philosophy than a programme (Roth et al, 2000). Eck and Rosenbaum (1994, p3) describe community policing as a 'plastic concept'; Fielding (2005, p460) calls it a 'chameleon'; Tilley describes it as 'slippery' (2008, p101). As early as 1988, Bayley warned that 'community policing on the ground often seems less a program than a set of aspirations wrapped in a slogan' (Bayley, 1988).

These definitional difficulties stem in part from the way that community policing has developed in different jurisdictions to answer different problems. While the essence of the model is to reconnect the police with the public they serve, both the issues that need overcoming and the ways in which relationships are built differ between localities, and need to be adapted to the particular needs of given communities. The ambiguity of community policing is therefore best thought of as a feature rather than a bug.

It is easier to describe what community policing isn't. It is often presented as a model that stands in counterpoint to reactive, response policing, a reconnection with 'traditional' modes of policing, as opposed to the 'professional' model that developed in the 1960s and 1970s (Skogan, 2008). This latter model had seen a disconnect between the state as the provider of services and the public as the recipients (Crawford, 1999, p23).

In the US, this was a deliberate move; the 'professionalisation' of policing was seen as a way of undermining 'strong ties' (Granovetter, 1973) between officers and their communities that could lead to corruption, and particularly close links between police and local politicians. These new 'professional' police departments were characterised by centralisation; a belief in their own expertise; autonomy from external influences; and a bureaucratic structure supported by modern technology (Uchida, 1993).

Similar processes of centralisation, professionalisation and specialisation led to the implementation of Unit Beat Policing in the UK. In the atmosphere of Wilson's 'white heat of technology' (Wilson, 1963), forces rushed to adopt two major technological transformations: the radio; and the fast patrol car, which allowed officers to patrol in Panda cars rather than walking the beat.

This reflected and reinforced a recurring strand in traditional accounts of police culture – a desire for action (Reiner, 2010). However, while officers enjoyed the glamour and dynamism of this new mode of policing, they gradually found themselves alienated from the ordinary routines of community life with which they had engaged while patrolling on foot: 'Fun and excitement, generated by the use of cars and radios, [has] replaced the cup of tea and chat in the local shop' (Holdaway, 1977, p126).

The turn towards community policing had several catalysts. In the US, deteriorating relationships between police and Black communities prompted innovative police leaders to explore new approaches. Perhaps the most influential was CAPS, which began in 1993. This saw teams of officers assigned on a long-term basis to small local beats, with systematic problem-solving processes and monthly 'beat meetings' (Skogan and Steiner, 2004). Patrol cars were reassigned to respond to 911 calls to free up officers' time, while extra civilian staff took on back office roles (Lombardo et al, 2010). With positive immediate results, the programme was highly influential in the development of community policing, both in the US and abroad.

In the UK, community policing had several drivers. Some of these came from within – for example, Chief Constable John Alderson in Devon and Cornwall believed that the sources of crime lay in deeper social conditions, requiring proactive policing, the identification of social problems and work with other agencies (Alderson, 1979). His books represented an important internal impetus for the serious consideration of alternatives to the existing models of policing (Savage, 2007a). Senior officers may also have seen the pluralisation of policing in the late 1990s as a threat; the private sector could increasingly take over local patrol functions if the police service was not seen to be taking this role seriously (Johnston, 2003; Innes, 2005a).

It was the Brixton Riots of 1981 which eventually provided what Tilley (2008, p98) calls the necessary 'spark' for community policing in the UK. The riots had their roots in the lack of trust between police and the largely Black community in this deprived area of south London, exacerbated by a police decision to increase 'stop and searches' in the area. A misunderstanding over an officer's attempt to take a young Black man who had been stabbed to hospital led to tensions finally erupting in April 1981. Some 300 police officers were injured and nearly 150 premises were damaged, looted or burned.

The Scarman report (1982) that followed argued that the disorder was in part prompted by policing that was focused too much on law enforcement, and which had actively damaged relationships with the community (Scarman, 1982; Savage, 2007a). It became the focus for a profound change in thinking around policing (Reiner, 2010). Scarman explicitly referred back to Mayne's 1829 instructions to the Metropolitan Police, arguing that the police responsibility to preserve public tranquility was more important than strict law enforcement. Scarman's two main conclusions were firstly that the 'community' needed to be involved in the development of policing policy and in the planning of operations, and secondly that police authorities needed to become more muscular, and could do so through new consultative arrangements.

The shift towards community-focused strategies was not immediate. The Conservative government of 1979, far from looking for a new way of connecting with citizens, responded to the Brixton and Toxteth rioting by calling for tougher tactics and equipment including water cannon (Reiner, 2010). Nevertheless, by the late 1980s, Scarman's ideas had become embedded in police thinking: the 'predominate conception of policing philosophy' among chief constables (Reiner, 2010, p246).

Arguably, however, the most important impetus behind what is now recognised as neighbourhood policing in the UK was the philosophical and political position of the New Labour government that came to power in 1997 – a theme developed further in the next chapter. This saw the desire to encourage police engagement with the public formalised into the Neighbourhood Policing Programme (NPP) that was rolled out from 2005 to 2008. The details of the development of the NPP, from its early manifestations as the National Reassurance Policing Programme through to the three-year programme itself, are dealt with in Chapter 3.

In the UK, neighbourhood policing has remained at the heart of policing practice despite the end of the original project in 2008, though it has since evolved under pressure of austerity-led budget cuts and the varying needs of different forces (Higgins, 2018). For the purposes of this book, community policing describes a general philosophy and set of programmes implemented internationally; neighbourhood policing is the type of community policing that has operated in the UK from 2005 onwards, in all its current diversity.

Issues with community policing

Community and neighbourhood policing have faced some resistance. Some of this has come from scholars, as well as from the police themselves. Critics argue that the definitional issues already mentioned are a major weakness (Mastrofski, 2006): if it is not clear what community policing includes, then how can anyone know it is being undertaken properly, or assess its success? A related issue is how community is defined, a concept rarely articulated clearly, while communities rarely match the clear geographical borders by which policing itself is organised (Tilley, 2008).

A second critique warns that the expansion in police numbers that community policing requires can mean an unsustainable expansion of the policing remit (Millie, 2013). From this perspective, the austerity-driven budget cuts of the 2010s offered an opportunity for policing to refocus on core tasks – but this opportunity risked being missed through the populist idea that 'front-line' policing should be protected at all costs. Instead, policing should relinquish many of the preventative elements of the community policing model, instead focusing on a smaller number of core policing tasks. This argument is revisited in the conclusion.

Another objection is raised by those who believe that the police role is inherently constrained in ways that make good community work difficult. For example, any demand for transparency between the police and the public is always going to run up against the limitations of police information sharing, while the responsiveness of officers is necessarily limited by their own powers and the legal constraints within which they work. The 'form' of the police–public relationship (Simmel, 2009; Harkin, 2015) also constrains partnership working: it is not clear the extent to which the police can construct with partners the kind of collective purpose and identity required to successfully work together (Harkin, 2015). Similarly, relationships between the police and the public are structured by the coercive capacity of officers to demand things from citizens – the public must serve officers just as the police serve the public (Tilley, 2008).

Resistance has also come from the police themselves. Officers can dismiss community policing as not 'real' policing. One early trial of neighbourhood policing in the 1980s was believed to have failed largely because of internal rebellion among officers themselves (Irving, 1986); officers rejected the philosophy and regarded these roles as low-status. This fits with other early literature on community policing that records significant cultural resistance to community policing (Myhill, 2006). Culture is particularly important where a model is more philosophical than programmatic as its implementation depends more on officers adopting those values (Mastrofski, 2006).

However, as community policing has been embedded in practice in many Western countries, this attitude has changed. Community policing can be reframed by officers to fit into traditional ideas of what 'real policing' looks like (Davies and Thomas, 2008). More importantly, as neighbourhood policing has developed, it is increasingly identified as 'real' police work (Higgins, 2018). In fact, one of the identified problems of neighbourhood policing nationally is that it has become so beneficial for officers' promotion prospects that many officers enthusiastically take it up for a year or so before moving on (Higgins, 2018).

Nevertheless, there are differences between what officers in front-line roles value, and the organisational values espoused by the force. It can be the case that the philosophy of neighbourhood or community policing is fully adopted by local officers – and at the same time that the organisation is increasingly focused on a different set of values such as risk and harm (O'Reilly, 2023) – a theme returned to throughout this book. Similarly, police organisations can struggle, particularly in a wider context of reduced budgets, with models such as community policing that produce outputs that lag over time or that are difficult to measure.

The final problem with the community within community policing is that it assumes that the community wants to be policed. Some have noted a particular reluctance on the part of the community towards such models in high crime neighbourhoods. Tilley (2008) suggests that effective community policing relies on an effective community, with compatible values, a shared identity and common understandings of key issues, such as how shared public space should be used.

Community policing models have also been considerably less successful in the Global South. Historically, most of the evidence on community policing strategies has come from the Global North. However, where evidence as to the efficacy of such strategies in the Global South exists, it suggests that there is much less of an effect on crime, disorder, fear of crime or police legitimacy. For example, a 2021 study that carried out six coordinated field experiments across Brazil, Colombia, Liberia, Pakistan, the Philippines and Uganda found no improvements in trust and no reductions in crime (Blair et al, 2021). However, the authors suggested that the findings might partly be explained by implementation issues, a lack of resources, frequently changing leadership, and police capacity and responsiveness, rather than hostility to the police presence by itself (Blair et al, 2021).

This underlines the variability of both structural conditions and local expectations. The demands of 'community' and the expectations of community policing vary widely. Imposing a model designed for one social context on a place where the prerequisites do not exist is a recipe for the failure of both the model and police legitimacy more widely. Evidence from post-conflict environments does suggest that some of the practices of community policing can be helpful – but they must be carefully tailored to local needs and acknowledge that, in the absence of a functioning and trusted state police service, many communities may have moved to a self-policing environment and see no purpose to the presence of the formal police: community policing structures may therefore need to support existing non-state forms of legitimate authority. Moreover, police officers in post-conflict environments may hold very different values to those that are embodied in community policing models of the Global North, and these cannot be effectively imported (Nilsson and Jonsson, 2023).

This context offers lessons to developed countries looking to refine their own policing models, and to practitioners considering how to implement or revitalise community or neighbourhood policing in their local areas. Police officers need first to understand what is already there: what structures exist, whose voices are heard, what community members value – and where they clash. This book will explore why all of this makes such a difference to the effective practice of neighbourhood policing, and will underline that it is never enough to simply label existing practice as community or neighbourhood policing, or to change its remit without consideration for its underlying purposes – that of supporting public confidence in policing.

Outline

This book begins by establishing the social and political context of neighbourhood policing in the UK. It argues that the model of neighbourhood policing instituted in the UK still bears the imprint of the New Labour government that came to power in 1997. This was manifested in ideas such as 'new localism' and the potential for public services to contribute to building communities. This, and the developing centrality of public confidence as a metric for measuring the success of the police, shaped the particular form which neighbourhood policing took in the UK.

The chapter then traces the changing context in which the neighbourhood policing model has operated, from the single confidence target of the late years of the Labour government, through the 'police as crime-fighters' philosophy of the Coalition that took power in 2010, and the effects of austerity on a model that by its nature was particularly vulnerable to budget pressures. It explores the 'fracturing' of the model (Higgins, 2018) and its repurposing to support a range of different priorities.

The second chapter picks up the theme of confidence as a core metric in neighbourhood policing, exploring the overlapping concepts of confidence and legitimacy. It discusses the considerable academic research into legitimacy and confidence, breaking down their definitions and what activities can support them or damage them. It also looks at demographic differences in levels of confidence in the police and assessments of police legitimacy. The chapter then looks at how this research was operationalised in the UK in the early trials of Reassurance Policing which evolved into the NPP, to show the extent to which the model was designed towards a specific set of mechanisms and outcomes. The chapter argues that the nature of public confidence and police legitimacy means that these mechanisms are still central to the effectiveness of the model, regardless of the other goals to which neighbourhood policing is now asked to contribute.

The next chapters look at three of these mechanisms. Chapter 4 looks at visibility and specifically at foot patrol. The chapter critically analyses both the resilience of public affection for police patrolling on foot and the evidence of its efficacy, both in reducing crime and providing reassurance – as well as whether other uniformed patrols are similarly effective. It then looks at other elements of 'visibility', such as the accessibility of officers to the communities they serve and their familiarity, both to residents and with the locality. The chapter argues that the value and therefore the purpose of visible police foot patrols should be seen in the context of the 'expressive nature' of public confidence, as well as its effectiveness, when targeted, in reducing crime and disorder.

Chapter 5 explores community engagement and begins by outlining the entrenchment in legislation and formal guidance of the need for the police to engage with the public. It discusses the different types of engagement and the tenacity of the public meeting despite its recognised disadvantages. The chapter explores the evidence supporting various types of engagement between the police and the public, and what problems are recognised with these, as well as what is known to support public confidence effectively. It also looks beyond direct engagement to how neighbourhood police teams can communicate with the public, including through virtual meetings and social media.

This latter theme is one that is picked up in Chapter 6, which focuses on problem-solving. It begins with a discussion of what 'problems' mean in the context of neighbourhood policing and the development of problem-oriented policing (Goldstein, 1990) as a policing model, and the differences between this and problem-solving within neighbourhood policing. It examines the dominance of SARA (scanning, analysis, response, assessment) as a model of problem-solving in the UK and looks at the problems with solving problems, including the difficulties in institutionalising both the practice of problem-solving and the necessary training and organisational support; the need to manage expectations, particularly in a contemporary context; and the limits of police capacity to resolve issues outside police remits.

This then segues to Chapter 7, which discusses partnerships in neighbourhood policing. This chapter begins with an outline of the recent history of partnership working in policing. It outlines and critically analyses government policy in this area, using this context to frame current guidance and best practice in partnership working – and notes the difficulties for forces in mapping and managing a complex constellation of statutory and non-statutory partners, operating at a multiplicity of levels. This in turn contextualises an examination of the evidence on what best supports effective partnership working and the potential for co-production with partners and communities, as well as critically interrogating this concept in the policing context and the limitations of both partnerships and co-production given the particular 'form' (Simmel, 2009) that police work takes. This chapter also outlines the way that public servants such as the police deal with value conflicts in partnership work, and warns of the danger of the police tendency to default to police values.

Chapter 8 explores the wider possibilities for local policing models. Early hopes for neighbourhood policing included that it might contribute to building stronger, more effective communities. This chapter looks at that promise and the evidence around social capital, collective efficacy and the ways that policing can contribute to these. It also looks at arguments that, in complex urban communities, collective efficacy and informal social control might be reflected in an increased willingness to call the police, rather than to directly intervene. The chapter looks at some emerging models for developing the relationship between police forces and the communities they serve, but also the arguments that the police remit is already too broad.

The final chapter brings together the themes developed in the rest of the book and looks to the future. This discussion highlights the importance of both the policy landscape and the internal strategic focus of the police at a national and force level. It argues that the current policy landscape from the perspective of both leading parties offers some encouragement to neighbourhood policing as a model. However, it also notes that policing has yet to refocus from the austerity-driven reprioritisation that saw harm and vulnerability take precedence over public confidence in policing. This unmooring of neighbourhood policing from its original purposes risks leaving it without the organisational support needed for the model to function effectively. Policing is under constant tension between its law enforcement imperative and the need to legitimate that capacity for coercive force; the final section argues that this can only be maintained through an understanding of the importance of relationships in policing, with partners and with communities.

How to use this book

This book can be approached in a number of different ways. It can be read as a critical analysis and narrative, taking the reader from the earliest inception of community policing and its flourishing in the CAPS programme, through to the contemporary challenges that the model faces and the possibilities for its revitalisation.

Alternatively, it can be read as a guide to neighbourhood policing in theory and practice. The first two chapters outline the context of neighbourhood policing and then the theoretical arguments as to why it works. Each of the later chapters offers an exploration of the evidence as to which activities work for neighbourhood policing and to what extent. Each chapter also offers some questions for consideration and suggestions for further reading.

Finally, a note on terminology: the NPP was a three-year programme that ran from 2005 to 2008. What is referred to, uncapitalised, as 'neighbourhood policing' is a UK model of policing which has in some cases significantly diverged from that original programme. Community policing – as discussed earlier – is a broad term, which describes a general philosophy and set of programmes implemented internationally; neighbourhood policing is the type of community policing that operates in the UK and was based on that original programme. This is the model that this book explores.

2

Social and political context

Introduction

This chapter tells the story of why and how neighbourhood policing emerged in the UK, and how it ended up in the particular shape and form we now recognise. It is important to understand this – and, crucially, what purposes it was intended to serve – to explain why some of the changes it has experienced over the last decade have been so damaging.

This part of the story begins in the mid-1990s, in the last years of a fading Conservative government, and a reformed Labour Party. Then-Shadow Home Secretary, Tony Blair, thought the party needed to recognise and address the real damage that crime caused to working-class communities who still made up the core of the Labour vote – but also to acknowledge that crime could not be addressed simply by locking more people up. This chapter explores the philosophy that grounded New Labour's policy on the police and which eventually produced neighbourhood policing as a model. This context matters: it is only because of the particular things that New Labour believed were true about communities, about the public sector, and about crime and the police, that funding and legislation was brought in that facilitated and shaped the Neighbourhood Policing Programme (NPP). This in turn affects policing strategy and practice to the present day.

The chapter begins by looking at the new government's focus on localism, a departure from previous assumptions of how public sector services should be delivered. It then explores the particular outcome of this focus on New Labour's policies for crime and policing – especially when coupled with the government's 'What Works?' agenda to improve public services through delivering evidence-based changes. It then touches on the roots of confidence as a policing metric (a theme which will be developed further in Chapter 3), and how that policy led first to Reassurance Policing, and then to the NPP, which ran from 2005 to 2008.

Continuing the narrative, the chapter then moves to what happened after the end of the formal programme and, particularly, after the change of government in 2010. It looks at the current state of neighbourhood policing and examines how neighbourhood policing became institutionalised in the UK, despite the major reforms affecting policing in the early years of the Coalition government. These reforms included the advent of Police and Crime Commissioners (PCCs), the end of ring-fenced funding and the deep budget cuts known as 'austerity' that encouraged forces to reassess their strategic priorities. The chapter concludes that, while in many ways neighbourhood policing has shown itself to be a more resilient model than perhaps could have been expected, there remain some deep concerns around the way that budget cuts have undermined its core purpose – the support of public confidence in policing.

New Labour, new neighbourhoods

New Labour's policy ambitions represented a profound break from the old left thinking that had previously dominated the party. This new approach was rooted in the idea that traditional distinctions between the left and right in politics were no longer relevant. This was because of an increasingly globalised economy, where financial markets held enormous power to punish governments for radical economic policies.

Some have described the outlook of New Labour as more sociological than ideological. Rather than focusing on what the country ought to become, or how the state ought to behave, the party instead started from an observation of what the country was like right now, and what that meant for public policy in the immediate future (Finlayson, 1999). This new pragmatic account of British society observed that the public were much less deferential than they had been, and much more inclined to challenge traditional forms of authority (Clarke et al, 2007, p11). This meant that traditional bureaucratic ways of organising public services were likely to be less effective, as people were less likely to unquestioningly accept the authority of people like police officers. Instead, what was needed was a way of organising society that was more attuned to the demands of the prosperous masses – 'citizen-consumers' (Vidler and Clarke, 2005).

In New Labour's vision of Britain, voters weren't hungering for the return of a paternalistic state, which looked after them but restricted what they could do. However, neither did they want to be completely exposed to the free market. Instead, there existed a political gap for a 'radical centre' in which policy started with what was most local to citizens. This 'new localism' was intended as a profound reconstitution of how governments should look at society and how services should be provided. Instead of the state being 'rolled back', as the previous Conservative government had attempted, or the state returning as the dominant provider of public services, as 'Old Labour' principles demanded, it was instead to become an enabler. This meant it would facilitate the provision of services in the shape that local people needed from a multitude of different sources, including public, private and third sector. This opened up new possibilities for the provision of public services, including the police.

In similarly radical fashion, the traditional Labour commitment to equality of outcomes was quietly abandoned in favour of ideas around social inclusion and exclusion. Previously, the left had focused on the way that the structure of society tended to reinforce economic inequalities, which then led to inequity in things like education and crime – both for victims and perpetrators. Social exclusion as an idea instead spoke to people's relationships – to each other and their communities – rather than their income alone, and policies aimed at increasing social inclusion could not be supported solely by tax policies aimed at redistributing wealth.

This was reinforced by ideas around social capital – which will be explored further in Chapter 8 – that suggested that people's active participation in public services was beneficial both to those services and those participating (Bochel et al, 2008). The central idea was that local people would take more responsibility for their communities, their local services and their own lives, and by doing so, would improve all three.

Casting residents as 'citizen-consumers' rather than subjects of the state meant they had to be entitled to a choice in their services as far as possible, and were in turn regarded as law-abiding citizens who wanted to actively contribute to the public good. Some scholars raised concerns that this vision automatically excluded people who weren't able to participate, or simply didn't want to. They warned that policy based on participation could reproduce existing patterns of inequality and power. The 'active citizens' that New Labour wanted to engage were much more likely to be produced in communities where people were already happy to engage with the state – middle class and well-educated (Hope, 2005). This was particularly worrying in the context of policing, given that criminologists had already observed a gap between those who felt comfortable calling on the police to protect them and those citizens who did not.

Nevertheless, this New Labour focus on the local, and its belief in the benefits of public participation in government, was applied across the public sector. While it took some time for policing to be fully incorporated into this 'new localism,' it was this vision of neighbourhood as the centre of citizenship that eventually underpinned the development of neighbourhood policing.

Police policy

New Labour's approach to policing policy was years in the making, and its mantra, 'tough on crime, tough on the causes of crime', formed a central part of its election campaigning. Part of this was simple statecraft (Buller and James, 2012): crime and law and order had long been seen as an area where the Conservative Party was strongest, meaning it had to be neutralised as an issue (Downes and Morgan, 1997). New Labour's policy on crime was designed to address both crime and the underlying factors behind crime: 'to make police and criminal justice agents of social integration' (Loader and Sparks, 2012, p26). This reflected an understanding that how people felt about crime mattered, and good law and order policy both addressed crime itself and people's subjective experiences of safety and the police.

New Labour's early policies on crime are sometimes, and with some justice, described as punitive and performance-obsessed (Brownlee, 1998). A combination of the party's pragmatic approach to policy, and a related desire to establish and respond to a clear evidence base, meant that the early years of New Labour's policing policy were characterised most strongly by performance management and targets, and what became known as the 'What Works?' approach to criminal justice. This began with an attempt to identify public needs. For demand to be managed, it first had to be identified; and public expectations 'dampened' through greatly expanded information about police performance (Fleming and McLaughlin, 2012, p283).

However, the imposition of such a wide range of targets began to limit police flexibility, as well as prompting extensive criticism from the police and from commentators. More importantly to the pragmatic and politically focused administration, public confidence was not increasing in line with reductions in crime. The publication of the Green Paper *Policing: Building safer communities together* in November 2003 (Home Office, 2003) was in part an acknowledgement of 'audit overload' (McLaughlin, 2005) and a sense that targets were too rigid to allow forces to respond to local needs. Instead, as the subsequent White Paper underlined, policing was to follow other public services in prioritising local needs, consumer voice and choice.

To do this it had to build partnerships with other agencies and local communities, and offer accountability at a local level. The new Community Safety Partnerships, introduced under the Crime and Disorder Act 1998, required a range of agencies to develop and audit local crime and disorder strategies (a theme picked up further in Chapter 7). This was a formal acknowledgement that many of the causes and the consequences of crime fell outside the realm of the police (Crawford, 2001). New members of the 'policing family' were introduced in the shape of Police Community Support Officers (PCSOs) in 2002; a reflection of the government's belief that services should be delivered by whoever was best positioned to do so, regardless of their statutory function or powers.

The final element in this landscape from within which neighbourhood policing was to emerge was communities themselves. The New Labour government believed in the capacity of policing to build stronger communities, and the 2004 White Paper underlined this. Residents were to contribute in a range of ways, from 'active citizenship' to formal priority-setting, in order to build a community that 'upholds basic standards of decency and is strong enough to prevent and deter offending' (Home Office, 2004b, p38). Thus the processes of local policing were clearly understood as contributing to informal social control and collective efficacy (ideas explored further in Chapter 8), as well as improving confidence in the police.

Confidence and the Neighbourhood Policing Programme

New Labour came to power in the middle of an extended period from the mid-1990s in which public perceptions of policing did not seem to be reflecting a decline in crime. In the early 2000s, the public tended to believe that crime was rising both in their local areas and in the country as a whole (Innes and Fielding, 2002). This became known as the 'reassurance gap', after an Association of Chief Police Officers paper, 'Civility First' (ACPO, 2001, cited in Tuffin et al, 2006). This gradually led to a shift away from intelligence-led policing models to community models (Innes, 2005a) and an increasing preoccupation with measuring public confidence in the police.

Confidence is a metric that for some time held a central place in British policing, and still retains considerable influence. Public trust or confidence in the police has a lot of benefits. It makes it more likely that the public will engage with the police, and that the police can be held locally accountable (Rix et al, 2009). It has the potential to support legitimacy in other ways too: if citizens engage with the police, then officers can be allocated more fairly because forces know where the problems are. Where citizens do not trust the police and therefore do not engage, forces may be unaware of ongoing problems, and can be perceived as refusing to send police where they are needed. The more the public have confidence in the police, the more likely they are to behave in ways that assume that officers can be trusted, such as calling them when there is a problem, being prepared to give witness statements, and passing them intelligence. This in turn lets the police behave in more fair and effective ways – a virtuous circle of these 'moment-to-moment acts of consent, compliance and cooperation' (Bradford et al, 2009a, p1). We explore the nature of public confidence in the police further in the next chapter.

To build public confidence, and in line with the 'What Works?' philosophy, the government turned to the evidence that had emerged from a project known as the National Reassurance Policing Programme (NRPP). The details of this are also explored further in the next chapter. At the heart of this was what was known as the 'signal crimes' perspective (Innes, 2004). This perspective suggested that some crimes mattered to communities more than others, because of the 'signals' they sent out about people's safety and the security of the areas they lived in. This was more than just fear of crime but about social order in general. The early findings suggested that the three mechanisms of visibility, community engagement and problem-solving could support confidence, and that these benefits were long-term (Quinton and Morris, 2008); supporting the roll-out of a similar programme on a national level to improve public confidence, feelings of safety, and improvements in crime and anti-social behaviour (Tuffin et al, 2006).

The three-year NPP that followed the NRPP was therefore an evolution of reassurance policing that happily coincided with existing internal and external drivers of police reform. The NPP hoped to build on the NRPP's findings, doing so through the delivery mechanisms of visibility, engagement and problem-solving, and was aimed not at directly reducing crime rates, but focusing on crime and disorder that mattered to local residents, which might include issues that were not crimes (Quinton and Morris, 2008). From the outset, therefore, neighbourhood policing in the UK was directly aimed at supporting confidence and perceptions of safety, rather than lowering crime rates.

With the end of the formal programme in 2008, there was an increasing emphasis on community engagement and public confidence in policing more generally (Longstaff et al, 2015). The introduction of a single target for police forces, that of public confidence, reflected this emphasis. Nevertheless, the Home Office's 2008 Green Paper noted that the confidence gap had still not closed. The Green Paper therefore committed the government to a new Policing Pledge. This included promises that the police would arrange monthly meetings with the public in every neighbourhood and reinforced the government's developing focus on accountability. The follow-up 2009 White Paper, *Protecting the public: Supporting the police to succeed*, saw the introduction of a 'Police Report Card', measuring performance on local crime and policing; satisfaction and confidence; protection from serious harm; and value for money. The focus was now a clear set of standards and 'a stronger right for the public to have a say in shaping local policing priorities' (Home Office, 2009, p8).

A year later, Labour lost the general election. The confidence target, and the policing pledge, were abolished by the incoming Coalition government in 2010. Neighbourhood policing itself, however, was not dismantled. Rather, individual PCCs were enjoined to make their own decisions about the relative weight that should be given to neighbourhood policing in the context of considerably straitened resources; the outcome of which is examined next.

The effects of austerity

In May 2010, the incumbent Labour government of Prime Minister Gordon Brown was defeated in a general election. The incoming Coalition government, made up of the Conservative Party and the Liberal Democrats, took office promising to reduce public spending, and reduce the budget deficit, having characterised the global economic crisis of 2007–2008 as an outcome of Labour profligacy (Stanley, 2016). This section will look at the priorities of the incoming government and how they were operationalised in terms of policing policy, and the effects this had on the neighbourhood policing model.

The first major element of change was the establishment of PCCs, representing a shift towards democracy as a way of ensuring accountability.

Along with later moves to devolve powers to regional elected mayors, this was intended on the surface to address concerns of a democratic deficit in police oversight and a perceived lack of input from local people (Almandras et al, 2010). However, the scrutiny mechanisms set up to hold the commissioners themselves to account were left toothless (Lister, 2014), meaning the four-year elections remained the only real mechanism of accountability. Given the very low turnout in elections, the democratic benefit of PCCs is arguable. However, they were an effective way of devolving responsibility for difficult decisions forced on forces by the deep cuts to budgets which followed.

Initially there were fears that PCCs would be populists who would 'politicise' the police, and there were strenuous efforts to present the role as attractive to independent candidates. However, this met with mixed results. In the early years, definite political distinctions emerged: while nearly 70 per cent of successful Labour candidates pledged to safeguard neighbourhood policing, just 10 per cent of successful Conservative candidates did so (Lister and Rowe, 2015). By the second round of elections in 2016, independent candidates had all but disappeared; indeed, at the time of writing there were no PCCs sitting as independents, and just one who was not a representative of the Conservative or Labour Party: Dafydd Llywelyn of Plaid Cymru, PCC for Dyfed-Powys. The main outcome for neighbourhood policing in the short term was the removal of ring-fenced funds for PCSOs, enabling decisions on this to be devolved to forces, and setting the scene for a fracturing of neighbourhood policing in terms of delivery (Higgins, 2018).

The second major policy change was the reduction in budgets under the umbrella of austerity, which involved cuts across the public sector. This was tied to a belief in the capacity of volunteers and the third sector to step up as part of the 'Big Society' to fill any gaps once the over-inflated state had been rolled back (Cameron, 2011). Unlike in the Thatcher years of the 1980s, the police were not exempted from these cuts. Instead, forces were regarded as having expanded their activities beyond their proper remit, as well as sitting on excessive reserves (May, 2015). Both of these were to be challenged.

This period also saw a renewed focus on law enforcement as the primary purpose of policing. The 'new orthodoxy' of the Coalition government (Reiner, 2013, p164) saw any tasks other than 'crime fighting' as extraneous duties from which the police needed to be liberated. Home Secretary Theresa May, addressing the Conservative Party Conference in October 2011, said: 'Some people question why we're reforming the police. For me, the reason is simple. We need them to be the tough, no-nonsense crime-fighters they signed up to become' (May, 2011). The Coalition government believed that cuts to budgets could be met by efficiencies in back-room functions, the withdrawal of police from activities beyond their remit, and the sale of bloated capital portfolios – police stations – without harming the capacity of forces to maintain front-line, 'crime-fighting' officers (*The Independent*, 2010).

The practical implications were severe, particularly for neighbourhood policing teams. Police numbers generally saw a steep drop, 14 per cent from 2009 to 2016, reversing all the expansion of the 2000s (Disney and Simpson, 2017). A reduction of 'back-room staff' was in some cases facilitated by mergers with other forces, but inevitably required 'front-line' officers to take on a wider range of tasks (HMIC, 2013). Local authorities meanwhile suffered up to 40 per cent budget cuts over the same period (Calver and Wainwright, 2018). This badly affected partnership working, as councils slashed their non-statutory functions, such as community safety and neighbourhood wardens, as well as cutting back in areas such as housing and social services.

Police forces were forced to reconsider what they could do with much more limited resources. This also prompted a re-examination at a strategic, national level of what policing should consider to be within its remit. A number of 'emerging problems' (CoP, 2017a, p15) began to take priority, such as child sexual exploitation and online crime. This initially emerged in a context of falling crime; a situation that subsequently changed, particularly with regard to violent crime. The House of Commons Select Committee for Home Affairs warned in 2018 that police were struggling to cope with these increased demands (House of Commons Home Affairs Committee, 2018). Some forces reacted by focusing on managing or suppressing that demand – on occasion, according to Her Majesty's Inspectorate of Constabulary (HMIC), to the extent of putting people at risk (HMIC, 2017, p8).

Many forces responded to these new challenges by prioritising areas of high risk and harm: the 're-imagining of the policing task' (Millie and Bullock, 2012). Several forces completely reconstituted their neighbourhood teams to focus their work on 'hidden harms' such as domestic abuse and hate crime (Higgins, 2018). However, 'hidden harms' take place behind closed doors rather than in the streets; they are crimes of private, rather than public, spaces (CoP, 2015a). While this was a sensible response to changes in demand – and particularly drops in volume crime – it also had the effect of devaluing subjective assessments of fear of crime, and therefore community input into setting police priorities.

All of this pushed policing away from seeing itself as a craft and towards searching for measurable outcomes based around harm and risk. Meanwhile there was also a renewed focus on 'professionalising' the police. The College of Policing was established in 2012 with a remit, in part, 'to ensure that policing practice and standards are based on knowledge, rather than custom and convention' (CoP, 2017b). The College introduced a new entry qualifications framework, arguing that the job of policing had become a complex profession requiring professional qualifications (CoP, 2017c). The change in strategic focus was also influenced by the launch in 2016 of the Cambridge Crime Harm Index (Sherman et al, 2016) and the adoption of a similar Crime Severity Score by the Office for National Statistics (Bangs, 2016).

HMIC warned in 2017 that this focus on risk, harm and vulnerability was in some areas critically undermining the provision of neighbourhood policing (HMIC, 2017). These changes in philosophy and in funding affected every aspect of policing, but neighbourhood policing was particularly exposed to these changes, as its focus on low-level and non-crime, on the importance of community determination of priorities, and on public confidence, stand in conflict both to a political philosophy that prioritises crime-fighting, and a strategic one focused on vulnerability and measurable harm.

The state of the neighbourhood

As early as 2013, it was clear that the pressures of austerity-driven budget cuts, and the force reorganisations that they had led to, were affecting neighbourhood policing on the ground. In 2013, the College of Policing decided to undertake a practice stocktake to examine the effects of three major changes on neighbourhood policing: spending cuts; the election of PCCs; and the loss of ring-fenced funding for PCSOs, which disappeared in 2013 when it was integrated into the Police Main Grant (CoP, 2015b).

The findings were striking. Of the 38 forces that responded to the survey, 32 had reviewed or were in the process of reviewing their local policing function. Of the 26 that had completed this process, half had made substantial changes to the organisation of local policing: 11 had integrated (or were planning to) their neighbourhood teams with other teams such as response or the Criminal Investigation Department. Two had given PCSOs sole responsibility for wards. Many had decided to redefine neighbourhood policing, to try to improve efficiency and give 'better value for money' (CoP, 2015b, p9), and had created new guidance for teams as to their tasks and purpose.

Similarly, HMIC's 2016 PEEL (police efficiency, effectiveness and legitimacy) report on police effectiveness found a 'varied and inconsistent' set of approaches to local policing. It identified just 25 forces of 43 that retained any dedicated neighbourhood model, in which officers spent their time on engagement, problem-solving and prevention (HMIC, 2017, p29). The Police Foundation found an even more fragmented set of approaches (Higgins, 2017, p2). The report identified five broad 'types' of neighbourhood policing in the UK, with the percentage of workforce in neighbourhood roles ranging from around 3 per cent to as much as 37 per cent.

The changes to neighbourhood policing since 2010 can be broken down into three overlapping categories: structure, capacity and purpose. As early as 2013, as noted earlier, a significant number of forces had begun to change the internal structure of their organisation in ways that affected neighbourhood policing. HMIC found that, by 2016, 17 forces had moved away from dedicated neighbourhood models; and the Inspectorate and expressed concern over the shifting away of resources from neighbourhood teams to give priority to addressing vulnerability and risk (HMIC, 2017, pp28–29). Many of these new models were hybrids of neighbourhood and response functions. However, several forces reported that the hybrid models had failed to deliver their intended outcome, often because the weight of demand meant that neighbourhood officers were 'pulled' towards response (Higgins, 2018). The Police Foundation report concluded that workload models with significant amounts of reactive work were simply unsuited to delivering neighbourhood policing (Higgins, 2018, p42).

Across the board, neighbourhood policing teams were also losing capacity. The Police Foundation found that the vast majority of respondents spoke of a significant deterioration of capability, despite official head counts suggesting that neighbourhood allocations had remained robust (Higgins, 2017, p27). Expanded responsibilities were, as with hybrid models, crowding out officers' capacity to undertake the long-term, consistent work needed to do effective problem-solving and other proactive work. Andy Higgins, author of the Police Foundation report, described this as a ' "perfect storm" of increasing workload and shrinking resource' (Higgins, 2018, p27). Both HMIC and the Police Foundation also noted the problems with increasing abstraction – neighbourhood officers being taken away from their work to deal with more immediate priorities. HMIC found 'very limited evidence of any assessment or understanding of the effect that taking officers away was having' (Higgins, 2018, p30).

Finally, neighbourhood policing was also losing its distinct sense of purpose. The College's practice stocktake found that the majority of the forces that responded identified a need 'to design service against demand' (CoP, 2015b, p11). The *Policing vision 2025* (APCC and NPCC, 2016) notably did not mention neighbourhood policing, referring instead to local policing, and acknowledging the imperative for policing to address rising demand. Across the board, neighbourhood policing had begun to shift its focus 'from providing reassurance to preventing/reducing crime, demand and harm' (Higgins, 2018, p33), with forces themselves expressing concern that confidence-building activities such as high-visibility patrolling were being pushed out by other force priorities. Understandings of problem-solving were changing from community-driven issues to case-based working around high-risk individuals (Higgins, 2018); and visibility was falling. A report from the House of Commons Home Affairs Select Committee (House of Commons Home Affairs Committee, 2018) warned that some forces' neighbourhood offerings had become little more than the co-location of multi-agency teams.

It was within this context that HMIC's landmark report was published. Concerned at the deterioration it observed, it recommended the College of Policing draw up new national guidance on the 'essential elements' of neighbourhood policing (House of Commons Home Affairs Committee, 2018, p23) which all forces would be expected to provide. These elements included public engagement, problem-solving and partnership work; and it underlined the importance of neighbourhood policing's preventative function and its role tackling serious organised crime and extremism. All forces were expected to immediately review their neighbourhood policing approaches to ensure these guidelines were met.

The new College of Policing guidelines acknowledge that the context for neighbourhood policing has changed in important ways, particularly in terms of decreasing resources and escalating demand, and the 'increased reporting of crime in private spaces' (CoP, 2018a, p2). The guidelines also make a point of reflecting existing practice, rather than insisting on a return to the models that operated under earlier, more generous funding regimes. Nevertheless, the very existence of the guidelines underlines a fact that is easily overlooked: that despite enormous external pressures, and the absence of any central direction or funding, neighbourhood policing – albeit fragmented – not only survived as a model, but had been institutionalised, rhetorically at least, as the 'cornerstone' of British policing (HMIC, 2017). With the issuance of the College of Policing's 2018 guidelines, and the incorporation of community policing elements into the Policing Education Qualifications Framework curriculum, it is now fair to say that British policing has broadly absorbed the need for community models to play a central role.

Summary

This chapter has argued that the context of the late 1990s and early 2000s offered a unique landscape for the development and implementation of a model of neighbourhood policing that was effective at supporting confidence. Its effectiveness can be seen in the way that it has largely been institutionalised despite political and policy upheavals. However, this changed landscape presents challenges to the delivery of neighbourhood policing.

The development of neighbourhood policing in the UK can be seen as the expression of two competing purposes for policing: coercive law enforcement, and the need to legitimate that power. This obligation to legitimate sits alongside a range of promising outcomes for neighbourhood policing. These include reducing crime, but also of reducing the fear of crime and of increasing confidence. However, the limited measurability of these benefits, particularly in the short term, means that it can be a struggle to secure continued political support when the emphasis of national politics changes.

The electoral defeat of the Labour government took with it much of the supporting policy structure of neighbourhood policing. In a much harsher political environment, neighbourhood policing has had to be recast in terms of its capacity to support other force goals. Delivery has fractured and the model has faced challenges of structure, capacity and purpose. Confidence has receded, in every sense. Neighbourhood policing has been repackaged and repurposed as a mechanism for delivering work on vulnerability, hidden harms, counter-terrorism and organised crime.

However, the marginalisation of confidence as a guiding principle is a risky one. The next chapter explores the nature of police legitimacy and public confidence. Given this evidence, it seems unlikely that public confidence in policing can be generated as a happy by-product of work focused on hidden harms and vulnerability. Nor is there robust evidence that the targeted work encouraged by the new neighbourhood guidelines can fully replace the universal, visible presence that the original NPP called for (discussed further in Chapter 4).

In consequence, if confidence is an oil tanker (Bradford and Jackson, 2010), it may have begun its long turn a decade ago, and it may take a similar length of time to turn it around again. The next chapter looks more deeply at the idea of public confidence in policing, the overlapping idea of police legitimacy and the evidence around what supports them.

Questions for further consideration

1. How important is the policy environment – for example, the existence of a supportive government, engagement from other policy 'actors' – to the implementation of changes to policing? What are the implications of this?
2. Why might policing seem to cycle between a focus on law enforcement and a focus on legitimacy? Is it possible to break this cycle?

Further reading

Clarke, J., Newman, J., Smith, N., Vidler, E. and Westmarland, L. 2007. *Creating citizen-consumers: Changing publics and changing public services.* London: SAGE.

Higgins, A. 2018. *The future of neighbourhood policing.* London: The Police Foundation.

Savage, S.P. 2007a. *Police reform: Forces for change.* Oxford: Oxford University Press.

3

Understanding police legitimacy and public confidence

Introduction

Neighbourhood policing was a programme developed, like other models of community policing, to fix a problem – a distance and disconnection between the police and local communities that was seen by policy makers as undermining police legitimacy. Legitimacy is particularly important in the British model of 'policing by consent'. Without legitimacy, it is hard for the police to function, especially in the UK, where the police are largely unarmed.

Consent is a central idea in British policing – what Reiner (2009, p52) calls the 'animating idea of official discourse about British policing', one that still provides it with a 'legitimating philosophy' (McLaughlin, 2005). The idea of policing by consent can be traced through British policing history. Accounts of the establishment of the New Police in 1839 are laced with violence, often on the part of citizens and aimed towards the police. There was significant hostility and mistrust towards these new officials. The government made concerted efforts to try to gain the consent of the public to being policed: officers were issued with truncheons, rather than armed, and dressed in blue, rather than red, in order to distance them from the armed forces who had been responsible for massacres such as that at Peterloo.

These early confrontations underline that consent is variable, must be earned and is never complete. Policing by its nature is inherently conflict-ridden, always containing the threat of coercive force: no police force can ever be entirely legitimated, because somebody is always being policed (Reiner, 2009). Yet, nevertheless, the police have to try. Particularly in the British model, this ongoing effort to negotiate legitimacy is central to the police being able to achieve their purposes; without consent, policing as we recognise it could barely happen at all.

This chapter begins by exploring the state of police legitimacy today. It examines some of the most high-profile recent crises of legitimacy, by looking at what happened, why it matters and what story each of these incidents and the responses to them tells us about policing in Britain today, and the trajectory of public confidence.

There is significant overlap between confidence and police legitimacy, and the chapter moves on to establish what each of these terms means. It explores how police behaviour can support confidence and legitimacy, or damage them – but also the limits of that influence.

The chapter then looks at how confidence was 'operationalised' in the early days of neighbourhood policing. It begins by outlining the signal crime perspective, which first theorised a way that determining locally important issues, and policing for reassurance, could help support public confidence in policing. It then looks at how Reassurance Policing was developed into neighbourhood policing through pilot programmes which established the effectiveness of its constituent mechanisms – visibility, community engagement and problem-solving – and how those mechanisms were designed and tested.

The chapter concludes that the evidence around the mechanisms through which neighbourhood policing can support public confidence in policing remains sound. While arguments exist – as touched on in the last chapter – for changing what neighbourhood policing does, these are largely based on changes to organisational demand, capacity and priorities. These changes might well make neighbourhood policing support a wider range of organisational needs. However, if they undermine the capacity of neighbourhood policing to undertake the central activities needed to support public confidence, it stops being effective neighbourhood policing.

A crisis of legitimacy?

Are we facing an unprecedented crisis in police legitimacy? To read the news headlines you might feel that the answer to the latter question is obviously yes. Yet the same question could have been asked at almost any point in the last 50 years and received the same answer. Policing in the UK appears to be not just periodically engulfed in legitimacy crises, but almost constantly so.

At the time of writing, British policing has had in the last several years to cope with the COVID-19 pandemic; Black Lives Matter protests; the outcry over the handling of the vigil for Sarah Everard, killed by a serving Metropolitan Police officer; arguments over institutional racism and institutional corruption; the exposure of WhatsApp messages shared by police in Charing Cross suggesting fundamental issues around police culture; and several forces – including the Metropolitan Police Service (MPS) – being placed into special measures. Each of these moments of crisis exposes wider issues around policing in the UK.

The COVID-19 pandemic brought policing by consent and the difficulty of negotiating legitimacy to the forefront of daily life. Tasked with enforcing lockdown rules that were broadly supported by the population, but deeply controversial in the details (and among some groups), the police had to walk a careful line between enforcing the law and damaging their own legitimacy by doing so.

The government introduced two pieces of legislation early in 2020 to deal with the pandemic: the Coronavirus Act 2020 and the Health Protection (Coronavirus) Regulations, a statutory instrument made by the Secretary of State for Health and Social Care under the Public Health (Control of Disease) Act 1984. It was the latter Regulations that allowed the restriction of movement, and crucially, of gatherings in a public setting. These regulations listed the reasons why people could be outside their homes during lockdowns, and specified the penalties, including fines, that could be issued by police. However, many of the details of the regulations, including the reasons that people could leave their homes, changed several times over the course of the pandemic, and sometimes in different ways in different geographical areas. These constant changes brought particular difficulties for the police in their attempt to enforce the regulations (Sheldon, 2021). Moreover, many of the most contentious restrictions were issued to the public as ministerial guidance, not regulations – an issue even police officers became confused by (HMICFRS, 2021a). Many of the high-profile cases of apparent police over-reach appeared to stem from this confusion.

Police forces broadly decided to take an approach in which enforcement and the issuing of fixed penalty notices was a last resort. Instead, the priority was a 'Four Es' approach: Engage, Explain and Encourage, before Enforcing (Grace, 2020; HMICFRS, 2021a). This approach was aimed at supporting legitimacy, being based on demonstrating fairness (see more on this procedural justice in the next section), and avoiding a coercive law enforcement approach until all else had failed.

Legitimacy was the central issue throughout this period. If police legitimacy, and that of the state, is strong, citizens are more likely to obey the law (the details of which are explored further in the next section). In the case of COVID-19, this meant communities would be essentially self-policing and the spread of the virus would be limited. Where legitimacy was low, there was a risk that people would not comply with the restrictions, and therefore the virus would likely spread faster. Too much of a crackdown risked damaging police legitimacy and make it less likely that enforcement would be effective.

However, the pressure on police to enforce the law also brought other confrontations that challenged their legitimacy among particular groups. In May 2020, George Floyd was murdered by a police officer in the city of Minneapolis in the US. His death sparked a series of 'Black Lives Matter' protests in cities across the world. Large protests were staged in several cities in the UK, including outside the US Embassy in London. Despite the limits on public gatherings in place, forces decided to tolerate the Black Lives Matters protests and clashes at the protests were limited. There were just five arrests, of which three were for breaches of COVID-19 legislation, though media reports indicated many protesters were in breach of social distancing guidelines.

It is possible to argue that Floyd's death was the outcome of a particular set of race relations particular to the US; and there is no doubt that these do not translate exactly to the British experience. However, to focus on this is to miss the point: the protests spilled over because they resonated with understandings of how police treat people of colour in the UK as well.

One manifestation of the ongoing problem facing the police is disproportionality in Stop and Search. As of 2017, Black people were nine times more likely to be stopped and searched for drugs than White people; Stop and Search was cited as one of the reasons behind the 2011 riots (Lewis et al, 2011). Successive Home Secretaries have moved to reform Stop and Search; yet the disproportionality remains. There are a number of potential explanations for the disparity, some of which call on structural issues outside the control of the police, as well as those that blame issues of institutional racism within the service. However, regardless of the explanation, and of its value as an investigative tool, Stop and Search is problematic for legitimacy because of its disproportionality in practice. Legitimacy, as discussed in the next section, relies on perceptions.

It is not just Black and ethnic minority members of the public who can have issues with trusting the police. Women have also accused police of institutional misogyny, and of failing to take their concerns seriously. The COVID-19 pandemic brought these concerns into sharp focus with the murder of Sarah Everard by Wayne Couzens, a serving member of the MPS, in March 2021. In the wake of her death, a local group called 'Reclaim These Streets' (RTS) announced that it intended to hold a vigil in memory of Sarah Everard on Clapham Common.

Despite reports that local Lambeth police officers were receptive to allowing the protest (Stott et al, 2022), the MPS made the decision that the vigil would be illegal under existing COVID-19 restrictions, and refused to allow it to take place. RTS challenged the MPS at the High Court, but the ruling was ambiguous – while the court underlined the right to peaceful protest, it also ruled that the police had the power to prevent such gatherings for reasons of public health (HMICFRS, 2021b). The MPS interpreted this as reinforcement of its decision to ban the gathering; while the RTS believed that it was justification for it to go ahead (Stott et al, 2022). Moreover, by this stage the planned vigil had received sufficient publicity that the RTS felt it likely that people would gather whether it was an official event or not (Stott et al, 2022). However, under the threat of being fined, the official organisers withdrew.

This left a vacuum of leadership among those gathering, and therefore an absence of capacity to plan and manage the event, which, as predicted, saw people gather on the Common anyway. While through the afternoon this continued to be a peaceful and low-key gathering, and was policed as such, once it began to get dark, police officers decided to ask those attending the event to disperse. When this dispersal was not forthcoming, four women addressing the crowd from the bandstand were arrested. The following day, this police action was condemned almost universally, including by Mayor of London Sadiq Khan who demanded an urgent meeting with the MPS (Stott et al, 2022). Then-Home Secretary Priti Patel called footage of the arrests 'upsetting' and asked Her Majesty's Inspectorate of Constabulary and Fire and Rescue Services to undertake an inquiry.

The MPS appears to have found itself caught in a bind with regard to the Everard vigil – a situation exacerbated by the knowledge that it was an MPS officer who had committed the murder. While officers could reasonably point out that it was other MPS officers who caught Couzens and gathered evidence against him – and there is no doubt that the vast majority of officers were horrified by Couzens' actions – this left the police on particularly delicate ground with regard to policing the vigil. Instead of responding to this delicacy, the MPS proceeded in a rigid fashion, which was challenged by protesters who argued that the judgment of the High Court meant it was entirely a police choice not to allow a legal vigil.

It is clear that decision-makers in the MPS felt they were doing the right thing within the constraints placed upon them by policy makers, and that they felt undermined by the response of both Khan and Patel in the aftermath of the confrontation. However, it is equally clear that, though the response to the vigil wasn't particularly coercive, it did considerable damage to perceptions of police legitimacy. This damage was so great perhaps because it reflected beliefs that some women already held: that the police could not be trusted to protect women and their interests.

Thus three recent moments in British policing serve to highlight issues of legitimacy with important ramifications for police practice, which will be explored further in the rest of this chapter. The pandemic itself highlighted the difficulty for police in balancing the requirements of coercive enforcement of the law and maintaining legitimacy; the Black Lives Matters protests underscored that the roots of some of these issues are complex and long-standing; while the Sarah Everard vigil throws up the complexity of balancing political demands with local exigencies.

However, while this particular constellation of events shapes the landscape of police legitimacy in the UK at the time of writing, it is likely that at any point in time it would be possible to draw on similar examples to illustrate the dilemmas faced by the police in sustaining their legitimacy. The next sections will begin to explore the content of legitimacy as a concept, to understand what is known about how it works and how police practice can sustain it; before moving to explore the related idea of public confidence in the police and how neighbourhood policing can support it.

Understanding police legitimacy

Confidence and legitimacy are separate ideas, though they have a lot in common. Confidence, which is examined in the next section, is about whether the public trusts the police. Legitimacy, on the other hand, is about authority – the right of the police, granted by the public, to tell people what to do, and to expect people to obey them.

There is clearly a relationship between these concepts. For example, it is hard to fully trust a group of people if you also think they have no right to tell anyone what to do. Similarly, you may find yourself reluctant to obey the instructions of an officer if you don't trust the police in general. It is because of this mutual reinforcement that police hope to build legitimacy in part by gaining people's trust. However, to say that you mistrust the police – a prediction about their future behaviour (Bradford and Jackson, 2010) – is not quite the same as insisting they have no right to enforce the law – a statement about their right to authority. The concepts are distinct.

There is some debate about where the legitimacy of the police comes from. On the one hand, some argue that the roots of police legitimacy lie in broad social, economic and cultural processes. Reiner (2010), for example, makes the case that police legitimacy was high in the 1950s because of the inclusive economic consensus that existed in the post-war years, which led to the incorporation of the working classes into the political and economic institutions of British society.

The police attained 'almost universal acceptance' (Reiner, 2010, p68) in the context of a society that itself was relatively prosperous and consensual. On the whole, people were happy to entrust the government to administer the police; having recently emerged from a war, they were comfortable with hierarchy and deference to authority; and the particular structure of the British police – which operated with minimal use of force and was accountable to local sources of authority – served to support this. From this perspective, changes to police legitimacy are largely the result of wider social changes, and mostly beyond the power of the police to affect.

Another perspective argues that the police can and do affect their own legitimacy through the way that they behave. This perspective, which is usually based on ideas around 'procedural justice', has become something of a sub-discipline in its own right.

Procedural justice is about fair treatment; police legitimacy can be supported by ensuring that the police treat people fairly. One model of this is the 'group values relationship model', which says that the four key elements of procedural justice include voice, neutrality, respect and trustworthiness (Lind and Tyler, 1988; Goodman-Delahunty, 2010). 'Voice' is the idea that citizens will be listened to by the police; it has symbolic value as it signifies that residents are valued by the authorities. Neutrality is the idea that the police should be unbiased, and should show this through being consistent, open and even-handed. Respect is behaviour that acknowledges people's rights and treats them with dignity; and trustworthiness is the extent to which the public think that the police are honest and prioritise the interest of the community (Tyler, 2006).

This model grew from early work by Tom Tyler, who defined legitimacy as a circumstance in which people believe that police decisions are broadly right, and their directions ought to be followed (Tyler, 2006). Co-operation with the police could be influenced by people's beliefs about the police and the law: that is, they will be more co-operative if they believe that the law, and the people enforcing it, are legitimate. This is in contrast to an 'instrumental' model, in which people only help the police because they think it will help them, through reducing crime. In an instrumental model, it is police effectiveness that matters – cutting crime, regardless of how it is done. In a procedural justice model, how things are done is more important than the results of those actions.

Tyler's research, and much of what came later, suggested that when people encountered the police, procedural justice increased legitimacy regardless of those encounters' outcomes (Tyler, 2004, 2006; Tyler and Fagan, 2008). Tyler argues that, through procedurally just behaviour, the police are effectively telling those people that they are valued, included members of society; and that they are also showing that they share the same values as the community: 'moral alignment'. Unfair treatment excludes people from these identities, so they no longer feel they belong and do not want to comply with those norms (Bradford, 2014; Bradford et al, 2014).

However, it is not always clear that we share values and norms; or that there exist clear communities which we are members of, and to which the police can demonstrate they are morally aligned. Sometimes we are members of more than one community; some communities hold very different values to others. Some argue that this doesn't matter as we have enough values in common to tie us together – a 'thin' universal morality that can connect all our different 'thick', or particular, moralities (Walzer, 1994; Bottoms and Tankebe, 2012).

Based on this, Bottoms and Tankebe argue for a set of basic expectations of policing in a liberal democracy that underpins police legitimacy. These expectations include procedural justice – fair decision-making and treatment – but add fair allocation of policing and its outcomes (distributive justice), and also effectiveness – they argue that this is a value in its own right, a belief in the role of the police.

However, another way of looking at legitimacy is to prioritise the variability of values, and the importance of what Bottoms and Tankebe describe as the 'audience response' (Bottoms and Tankebe, 2012, p129). In this light, legitimacy is negotiated, it is an ongoing debate, and it will take different forms according to the social and political context of the discussion. From this perspective, what people consider 'fair' may be different according to time and place and experience.

Looking at legitimacy through this lens also allows the police to be included as a group with their own separate values and expectations, that sometimes differ in important ways from those of the wider public (Loftus, 2009; Reiner, 2010; Charman, 2017). Seeing the police in terms of a group allows the investigation of how other groups might identify with the police, or react to them, rather than simply seeing them as representatives of the state (Radburn and Stott, 2019).

All of this means that the legitimacy of the police is complex, but probably rests less on effectiveness and more on perceptions of fairness. It also means that certain kinds of behaviour can increase perceptions of fairness; but that to understand and respond to what communities see as fair, police have to communicate directly with them. For example, what the police see as a fair distribution of policing resources might not be the same as those of a community. Some might feel under-policed; others over-policed, by the same officers. This local social context is therefore vital to understand to build legitimacy – and, by association, trust and confidence, to which this chapter turns next.

Public confidence in policing

The close relationship between confidence and legitimacy means that sometimes the terms are used interchangeably. This can make it difficult to determine which idea we are talking about, or to work out how to measure how police behaviour can affect them. However, they are distinct. Confidence is usually assessed through survey measures asking respondents to rate the performance of their local police (Bradford, 2011). Until it suspended its public perceptions module in 2020 due to the COVID-19 pandemic, the Crime Survey of England and Wales (CSEW) regularly asked questions on public confidence in policing, and many forces continue to do so as well.

As with legitimacy, confidence appears to be under threat. Levels of public confidence in policing rose between 2006 and 2012, stabilised until around 2016, and since then have steadily fallen (Police Foundation, 2022). The Police Foundation's *Strategic review of policing* links these figures directly to the increase in neighbourhood police officers from 2005 to 2008 onwards, and the fall in confidence to the reduction in officer numbers during austerity (Police Foundation, 2022, pp50–51).

Confidence appears to be 'sticky' – indicators can take several years to shift after a major change. This stickiness, and the lag in confidence responding to changes in force organisation and numbers, may have reassured forces that reforms to neighbourhood policing were doing no real harm, and that public demand was changing in line with crime demand. This is an assumption that was clearly premature.

Though slow to change on a population level, confidence is fragile at the level of the individual. All contact with the police is much more likely to damage than to improve confidence, while unsatisfactory contacts are consistently shown to damage confidence (Skogan, 2006; Bradford et al, 2009b). This seems to be true regardless of whether contact is self-initiated (such as reporting a crime) or police-initiated (such as Stop and Search).

In particular, contacts with the police seem to damage perceptions of police effectiveness (Bradford et al, 2009b). This may be because many encounters initiated by citizens may be disappointing: police can rarely solve residents' issues as quickly and competently as they'd like. Low visibility also harms this aspect of confidence. The authors suggest this may be about how the police communicate their effectiveness; being seen on the beat is being seen to do the job 'properly', in the way that the public expect. Broadly, perceptions of effectiveness seem to be separate to overall confidence, and the smallest of the factors contributing to it — bad news for forces (and governments) that assume the main purpose of policing is to be seen to fight crime.

There are also demographic differences in levels of confidence in the police. For example, males are slightly more likely to be dissatisfied with the police. Similarly, younger people are much more likely to be unhappy with the police (Jackson and Sunshine, 2007). Asian residents in the UK have been traditionally more likely to regard their local police positively than White residents (Jackson and Bradford, 2009); however, in the last ten years, levels of confidence among Black residents have fallen (ONS, 2021).

However, positively received encounters can deliver small improvements to confidence, partly through perceptions of police fairness and community engagement (Bradford et al, 2009a). There is a lot of evidence to suggest that tackling low-level signs of disorder can improve public confidence (Dalgleish and Myhill, 2004; Innes and Roberts, 2008). Rix et al (2009) found four types of intervention that had shown improvements in confidence: high-quality community engagement; local communications; restorative justice; and neighbourhood or community policing. The first of these, high-quality community engagement, can include polite and respectful responses to the public, and making contact with residents while undertaking foot patrol (Bennett, 1991; Myhill and Beak, 2008), as well as the kind of active engagement work that became an explicit part of the Neighbourhood Policing Programme (NPP), discussed later in the chapter.

However, there is also evidence that social context is very influential in the extent to which citizens are prepared to trust the police (Bradford et al, 2018), and particularly their sense of community connection and attachment. Different neighbourhoods can respond in different ways both to disorder and to the police response: more cohesive, prosperous areas are more alert to disorder; but less cohesive neighbourhoods respond more to high-quality police–community engagement (Perkins, 2016). This suggests the police need to be aware of neighbourhood-level variations in response when planning confidence-improving interventions; a subject turned to next.

Overall, the evidence therefore suggests that confidence in policing, like legitimacy, is not just instrumental – based on self-motivated worries about being a victim or being afraid of crime – but instead stems from broader issues related to the police as an institution, and society, and social order, as a whole. Residents' concerns are about connection and civility: when asked about problems in their neighbourhood, people prioritise 'anti-social families' (30 per cent) and 'neighbours not knowing each other' (29 per cent) as being among the most significant (ICM Research, quoted in Clark and Taylor, 2014).

These 'expressive' concerns are rooted in broader anxieties about social change and civility in daily life. In this conception, trust in the police is also an expression of trust in social norms and belonging (Loader, 2006, p204). Confidence in the police is confidence in what the police stand for – the 'organised defence of the norms and social ties' (Jackson and Bradford, 2009, p499) that root people's social existence. Police officers being highly visible reinforces people's sense of stability and order, physically demonstrating that the 'authorities' the police represent haven't abandoned people's neighbourhoods (Giacomantonio et al, 2015).

This marries with the findings of the *Strategic review of policing* (Police Foundation, 2022). The review, drawing on data from the CSEW, suggests that there is a close relationship between confidence and 'indicators of community connection', which include measures of things like whether the police understand local concerns; whether they can be relied upon; and whether they actually deal with local issues. Confidence is much less clearly linked to perceptions of procedural justice like fair treatment and respectfulness. The review concludes that public confidence in policing is improved by the police systematically seeking to engage, listen and respond to local concerns (Police Foundation, 2022, p51) – all the functions of good neighbourhood policing. The next section explains more about why this might be the case.

The signal crimes perspective

One way of understanding why local engagement matters so much is to think about the differences between how different neighbourhoods understand and experience different types of crime and disorder. One of the first frameworks for doing this was the signal crimes perspective. Developed by academics at the University of Surrey (Innes and Fielding, 2002), this was a response to the observation that, despite drops in recorded crime, people's subjective sense of safety, and levels of fear, weren't falling in the same way. The signal crimes perspective was at the heart of the National Reassurance Policing Programme (NRPP), which eventually developed into the NPP (Innes et al, 2020).

The fundamental insight of the signal crimes perspective is that some crimes matter more to people than others. Some crimes have more effect on residents in the way that they shape their beliefs about their area and how safe they feel in their neighbourhoods. Some forms of crime and disorder can be overlooked – while others are 'signals' to residents that they need to be on their guard. This is not an objective assessment based on the levels of crime in a neighbourhood, but a subjective one; some apparently more serious incidents can be incorporated into residents' existing understandings of the world, while others are construed as warnings of future risk.

This understanding means that fear of crime may also be subjective and not directly related to actual risk of harm. Instead, 'fear of crime' might be a metaphor within which people articulate a wider set of anxieties about the social order and their place in it (Innes and Fielding, 2002) – just as the last section discussed the way that confidence in policing seems to be an expression of trust in that social order and the willingness and ability of the police to look after it. This also means that survey measures on fear of crime might not actually be measuring fear, so much as anger, annoyance or heightened awareness of crime and disorder in the local neighbourhood (Ditton et al, 1999; Farrall and Ditton, 1999; Hough, 2017). Even where signals of disorder are relatively weak, cumulative exposure to these could suggest a decline in order sufficient to generate a shift in people's confidence in their own safety.

If true, this has important ramifications for how the police should respond to communities when they raise concerns over objectively minor disorder. If forces interpret communities' concern over low-level crime as a sign of public ignorance, which could be improved through education or better information, then they are failing to understand the meanings that communities give to those incidents. Giving out more information about crime or trying to educate residents that their real risks are low, instead of alleviating those concerns, could underline this lack of understanding and demonstrate that the police are not addressing the issues that matter to local residents.

The second important element of the signal crimes perspective is that of local variability. For example, low-level disorder such as graffiti may not be remarkable in a neighbourhood that suffers from high crime and disorder in general; but it can be of real concern in a more orderly neighbourhood precisely because it is unusual. Moreover, this can differ within communities: the presence of graffiti may send different signals to younger people than to the elderly. Forces need to be aware therefore that the way crime and disorder is interpreted can be affected by the characteristics of residents as well as the 'situated context' of the crime or disorder (Innes and Fielding, 2002). This means that, to fully understand the context of community concerns, forces need to engage deeply at a local level. A reliance on local crime data will not be sufficient – some communities may be entirely unconcerned by issues that are a major anxiety for others.

Effective local policing should therefore focus on incidents that have a disproportionate effect on the public's perception of risk (Innes and Fielding, 2002). Interventions need to be high-profile – to send 'control signals' that communicate a message to the public that the police are taking protective action (Innes, 2004, 2005a). This could help harness the 'dramaturgical power' of the police capacity for formal social control (Innes, 2007, p133) and thus symbolise security for local residents (Barker, 2014). These ideas formed the heart of the NRPP, which was implemented in 16 wards across eight police forces (including the MPS) from October 2003 (Quinton and Morris, 2008).

A consensus had been building for some time around how policing had to change. Her Majesty's Inspectorate for Constabulary (HMIC) in its 2001 report 'Open all hours', had recommended that policing needed to increase its visibility, accessibility and familiarity to reassure residents and increase public confidence (Povey, 2001). This also reflected a recognition that communities had been stripped of the 'guardianship' of public sector stewards such as park-keepers and bus conductors (Innes, 2005a; Crawford, 2006). However, the evidence suggested that more was likely to be needed (Innes, 2005a, p161): systematic problem-solving, and partnerships with other agencies, given that so much of what communities wanted the police to do was likely beyond the police remit. This laid the ground for the establishment of the NRPP, followed in 2005 by the three-year NPP. The next section explores how these ideas, and the evidence to support them, was tested and integrated into local policing practice.

Theory into practice

The NRPP was trialled in 16 wards in eight police forces, including London, from October 2003. The NRPP was itself built on pilots run by Surrey police. The stated purpose of the NRPP was to reduce anti-social behaviour and improve quality of life, reduce fear of crime and improve people's sense of safety, increase public confidence and satisfaction in police, and improve social capacity (Quinton and Morris, 2008). These objectives were to be delivered through officers in the pilot areas focusing on foot patrol, community engagement and problem-solving.

The pilots saw neighbourhood policing introduced under controlled conditions, in small areas (local authority wards). This allowed the programme team to tightly control and monitor the intervention. Wards were chosen by the forces which decided to participate in the trial. However, there was an attempt to ensure that the 16 areas were drawn from a range of environments; for example, both rural and urban, and with different levels of prosperity or deprivation. Six sites were also matched with comparison sites with similar crime levels. Although, as Quinton and Morris (2008) note, these were hardly laboratory conditions, this close control lent credence to the outcomes.

The structure of the NRPP was based on the belief that the (re) introduction of visible authority figures into neighbourhoods would help facilitate community engagement with the police. This would be achieved through a systematic process of problem-solving, bringing in the community and partner agencies, to target police work towards the specific priorities of local residents (Quinton and Tuffin, 2007). A waterfall of outcomes was expected to ensue: from improvements in perceptions of crime and disorder to lower levels of fear and increased confidence and improved collective efficacy – the cohesiveness of a community and its capacity to self-police (discussed further in Chapter 8).

The NRPP was broadly successful in its aims. The programme improved perceptions of foot patrol; and increased perceptions of police visibility were associated with increased public confidence in the police. There was also a 12 per cent increase in the proportion of residents who knew their local police officers by name or by sight (Tuffin et al, 2006).

In terms of community engagement, there was an improvement across several measures, including perceptions of how much effort the police put in and how willing they were to listen to people's views (Quinton and Tuffin, 2007). These improved perceptions were also associated with improved public confidence (Quinton and Morris, 2008).

The NRPP also showed that problem-solving had significant potential to reduce crime in limited areas, especially if the community was involved; and that the public noticed such interventions, particularly around anti-social behaviour (Tuffin et al, 2006). Problem-solving in the NRPP was focused on incidents with a particular 'cognitive visibility' for the public – signal crimes (Innes, 2005b, p192); with sophisticated tools trialled to determine what these were.

Overall, the NRPP delivered increased confidence, lower victimisation, improved feelings of safety, perceptions of lower crime and anti-social behaviour, and greater community engagement, visibility and familiarity. There appeared to be clear and consistent links between the 'mechanisms' of visibility, engagement and problem-solving, and improvements in confidence, and most of these benefits were sustained over the longer term (Quinton and Morris, 2008). The evaluation therefore concluded that rolling out a programme of neighbourhood policing on a national level would likely deliver 'improvements in crime, public confidence, feelings of safety, fear of crime and perceptions of anti-social behaviour' (Tuffin et al, 2006, p93).

There were some important changes between the NRPP and the NPP (Innes et al, 2020). The roll-out of the NPP from 2005 was on a much greater scale – to 43 Basic Command Units at first, then across whole forces in its second year. This brought new problems with competing demands. There was also an element of 'rebranding' involved, from reassurance to neighbourhoods. The idea of 'neighbourhood' appealed to a desire for a shared identity based around geographic locality and common interest, as opposed to 'reassurance', which was complex, had multiple meanings and was more difficult for the wider public to immediately understand (Innes, 2005a).

However, by the end of the second year of the NRPP, programme effects for police visibility had fallen; the proportion of people across the sites, and particularly in London, reporting that they had seen an officer on foot patrol once a week or more fell. Perceptions of the police were still higher than at the start of the programme, leading Quinton and Morris (2008, p12) to conclude that in the long term, police visibility may be less important than the other identified mechanisms of community engagement and problem-solving.

By the launch of the NPP, 'improved perceptions of police effort in finding out what the public think' had been formalised into a list of critical success factors on three related vectors: public priorities, community engagement and communication (ACPO, 2006). These overlapped considerably with problem-solving; police were encouraged to go beyond public meetings to include street briefings, house to house calls and 'other innovative methods' (ACPO, 2006, p15), and to use community engagement to 'actively involve community participants in problem-solving processes'. However, the distinction between problems and signals, and the systematic approach to tackling signal crimes and disorders, had receded (Bullock, 2010).

The mechanisms of visibility, community engagement and problem-solving were therefore established. By the third year of the NPP, HMIC was able to say that 'all forces [had] achieved the basic standard of making sure that Neighbourhood Policing is a core part of policing work' (HMIC, 2008). As described in the last chapter, this basic shape persisted – though the mechanisms themselves have come under threat. The next few chapters explore further the nature of these mechanisms, how they work and what forces can do to employ them most effectively.

Summary

Legitimacy crises appear to be part of the nature of policing; a feature of the inevitable tension between officers' coercive, law enforcement powers, and the need for them to secure the consent of the population as a whole to being policed. Such consent is inevitably only ever partial. Recent crises have underlined that these issues are complex: the police are constrained by law, by expectations of enforcement and by the difficulty of ensuring fair treatment in a world that is broadly unfair in ways over which they have little influence.

However, points of tension can often be identified where marginalised groups are seeking a voice, and, while the police can do little to redress structural inequalities, some future legitimacy crises could perhaps be preempted through ensuring policing is at the front of the queue in terms of ensuring equity. Ways in which the police can promote equity include procedural justice – giving people a voice, treating them with respect, offering neutrality, and being honest and trustworthy. These behaviours can increase legitimacy through telling people in their encounters with police that they are valued members of society. If the police treat people fairly, they are more likely to cooperate with the police and obey the law.

However, perceptions of fairness can differ – different groups may have different ideas of what is fair, and judgements may also change according to what is happening on the ground. This underlines the importance of forces understanding what Radburn and Stott (2019) call the 'situational and cultural contingency' of these judgements. It is also important to see the police as a group in their own right, with their own subjective judgements of fairness which will differ at times from the judgements of those being policed. It may be particularly difficult for officers to recognise that their own judgements of what is right and fair may not be the only valid accounts. Legitimacy therefore needs to be seen as something that is an ongoing negotiation between officers and communities, and not something that can be taken for granted. Confidence in the police is similarly a social relationship, resting on expressive factors like perceptions of social order, and how visible and engaged the police are in the community. Confidence seems to be rooted in residents' perception of whether the police – and, by extension, the 'authorities' – are prepared to ensure local order – how safe people feel in their neighbourhoods, the extent to which they feel looked after rather than abandoned. This requires local police to systematically engage, listen and respond to local concerns.

It is clear that, in order to support legitimacy and public confidence, forces need to understand the particular needs and understandings of local residents. The signal crimes perspective explains more about why this is the case. Put simply, without talking to residents, officers can't know what types of incident act as signals of disorder, and what kind of response would be welcomed. Ignoring this local variability can lead to counterproductive strategies: for example, forces may rely on local crime data rather than community input, or try to 'educate' local residents as to why the issues that concern them are not high priorities, thereby underlining that they do not understand local concerns and risking damage to public confidence.

All of this was integral to the early versions of neighbourhood policing: the NRPP and the NPP that followed it. However, building on the last chapter, it is not clear that neighbourhood policing as a model continued to be organisationally valued under conditions of austerity. There may well be business case arguments to change what neighbourhood policing does, but these are not about making neighbourhood policing better. The risk is that neighbourhood policing is pursued as a model but with its internal mechanisms damaged or removed, leaving it unable to support confidence in the way that this chapter has outlined. The next chapters look more deeply at the working of these mechanisms to examine the case for each of them and what works best to support public confidence in policing.

Questions for further consideration

1. What are the major barriers in terms of resources and organisational culture to a focus on confidence and legitimacy?
2. Can you explain a recent crisis in policing in terms of confidence and legitimacy, using the definitions outlined in this chapter?

Further reading

Innes, M., Roberts, C., Innes, H. and Lowe, T. 2020. *Neighbourhood policing: The rise and fall of a policing model.* Oxford: Oxford University Press.
Mazerolle, L.G., Sargeant, E., Cherney, A., Bennett, S., Murphy, K. and Antrobus, E. 2014. *Procedural justice and legitimacy in policing.* Cham: Springer.
Police Foundation. 2022. *A new mode of protection: Final report of the strategic review of policing in England and Wales.* London: Police Foundation.
Reiner, R. 2010. *The politics of the police.* Oxford: Oxford University Press.

4

Visibility and foot patrol

Introduction

Police visibility has been an important part of rhetoric on law and order for successive governments. Visibility made up a large part of the Labour government's promises as outlined in its 2004 White Paper, *Building communities, beating crime*. Citizens were promised 'a more visible, accessible police presence on the streets and in their communities' (Home Office, 2004a, p8), and it formed a core part of the National Reassurance Policing Programme (NRPP). Even after the 2010 change of government, and the cuts to police budgets that followed, police visibility remained important, at least in principle: Theresa May's 2011 speech to the Conservative Party Conference, which announced the abolition of the single confidence target and insisted that the primary role of the police was 'cutting crime', also insisted that the police 'must remain visible and available to the public' (May, 2011).

As the last chapter laid out, visibility appears to be a key component in creating and sustaining public confidence in the police, although it may not be able to do this alone. Visibility appears to be part of a range of police activities that support confidence through reassuring the public that their neighbourhoods are safe and secure, and that this local order will be defended by the authorities; it is part of a kind of policing that reassures people that they matter, and they belong.

This chapter begins by looking at the enduring popularity of visible policing, and particularly of foot patrol, and the place in British culture of the 'bobby on the beat'. It does this by looking at the evidence that shows foot patrol to be more effective in supporting confidence than patrol in vehicles, and explaining this – and the seemingly endless demand for foot patrol – in the context of what it symbolises to the public.

We then examine research around the capacity of foot patrol to fight crime and disorder – in particular, the increasing evidence that targeted foot patrol can lead to small but significant reductions in crime in 'hot spots'. The chapter also looks at the importance of what the police do in these patrols, underlining the potential dangers of taking a purely law enforcement approach.

A broader idea of what visibility means also allows us to consider it in terms of the value of accessible and familiar policing to communities. Here the chapter looks at the shrinking number of police stations and what effect that is likely to have on public confidence, as well as the other ways that the public can access police services. We also explore the importance of public familiarity with individual officers, and of officers' familiarity with their local neighbourhoods.

Finally the chapter examines whether police visibility can be enhanced through non-warranted officers. This section examines the evidence around the benefits of engaging the 'wider police family' in neighbourhood policing, such as Police Community Support Officers (PCSOs) and neighbourhood wardens, and the potential issues that arise in doing so.

The chapter concludes that police visibility – and foot patrol in particular – retains its centrality in good neighbourhood policing practice, through supporting confidence, but also in reducing crime and disorder. It achieves these in three ways: through the symbolic presence and representation of order; through deterrence and guardianship, which is particularly effective through the use of targeted 'hot spots' patrol; and through enhanced local knowledge.

Popularity

The traditional image of the British police officer – uniformed, approachable, patrolling on foot – has a powerful hold on the public imagination. This can translate into an apparently relentless public demand for more 'bobbies on the beat'. This chapter therefore begins by looking at the place that visible policing holds in the public imagination and particularly the role played by the 'British bobby'. It explains the symbolic importance of foot patrol, and looks at the difficulties that this popularity throws up in terms of meeting the other demands of policing, which cannot be addressed through foot patrol alone.

It is difficult in the UK to disentangle public expectations about visible policing from the way that 'bobbies on the beat' have been used as symbols of policing, whether by politicians or the police themselves (Wakefield, 2007). Other countries also mythologise certain types of officers; for example, uniformed Mounties are used to symbolise Canada as a 'safe' state (Szczepaniak, 2007). However, the 'bobby' has become part of a cultural mythology of Englishness (Brunger, 2014). Images of British police officers in their familiar uniform and tall 'custodian' hats are so iconic that they appear on tourist souvenirs, while the now almost vanished blue police box has eternal cultural status thanks to Dr Who. It is an image associated with a nostalgic desire for officers who are 'friendly, familiar and trustworthy' (Wakefield, 2006, p10); the sort of police officers that can safely be approached to ask directions, or the time. The bobby on the beat represents 'consensus, community and order' (Loader, 1997, p15).

Although beat patrol was central to Peel's vision of the New Police in 1829 (Wakefield, 2006), the modern conception of the bobby was largely constructed through post-war imagery such as *Dixon of Dock Green*. In this, the police constable was presented as an essentially English figure: 'an uncomplicated, down to earth, seen-it-all London "bobby" who knows his "manor" inside out and who is called upon to deal with the everyday rather than serious crime' (McLaughlin, 2005, p17). This image of British police officers is entwined in the mythology of British policing with the Peelian principles, a set of tenets ascribed to the founder of modern policing but which more likely stemmed from early police textbooks of the 1950s (Lentz and Chaires, 2007). It is also an image that has also been cheerfully exploited by the Police Federation in ad campaigns to try to fend off government reforms (McLaughlin and Murji, 1998). The position of the 'British bobby' in the public imagination is in part a result of the actions of the police themselves in placing it there.

It has been effective. Most people in the UK still feel that visible policing in their area is important, and they want that policing to be on foot – 78 per cent thought it was important to see officers on foot patrol in 2018, though nearly four in ten had not seen an officer on foot at least once in the previous year (BMG Research, 2019). Nearly half were dissatisfied with the amount of foot patrol they had seen in their neighbourhood. Respondents believed that police visibility – whether on foot or in vehicles – acted as a deterrent and gave them peace of mind (BMG Research, 2019).

The symbolic value of visible policing is not confined to the UK. Research undertaken elsewhere has underlined the importance of foot patrol as part of a general service model of policing (Manning, 1997). There is consistent evidence that visibility and familiarity are successful ways of improving perceptions of the police (Pate et al, 1986; Skogan and Hartnett, 1997; Dalgleish and Myhill, 2004) and of boosting confidence (Zhao et al, 2002; Sindall and Sturgiss, 2013). Officers in the US were rated as more approachable, respectful and accountable when in uniform than not; and when on foot or bicycle than in a vehicle (Simpson, 2017). There is similar evidence from elsewhere in Europe to suggest that residents have better perceptions of police who patrol on foot compared to those they see patrolling in cars (Salmi et al, 2000).

The widespread public affection for foot patrol can perhaps be explained by thinking of patrol as a symbolic expression of the guardianship of the state and its authority (Waddington, 1999). People want to see the police in this approachable mode because it persuades them that their neighbourhoods are cared for and that they are all on the same side (Bradford, 2014). This visible, tangible presence of the police assures residents that local order in their neighbourhood is secure and so are they.

The desire for visible foot patrol is differentiated among different groups of the population; perhaps unsurprisingly, those most likely to demand the most visible patrolling are women and those over 60. Those most in favour of foot patrol see it as evidence that 'something is being done' and a powerful message of reassurance (Bradley, 1998, p10). It is often introduced or emphasised to achieve some element of 'reassurance'; raising visibility, accessibility, familiarity or improved local knowledge (Wakefield, 2007). However, younger people consider police visibility to be much less important than older people – a study by Her Majesty's Inspectorate of Constabulary for Scotland which focused on under-16s found that police visibility was not important to these young people at all, and that some younger residents found a police presence more likely to presage harassment than to be reassuring (HMICS, 2002).

Notwithstanding these variations, the public hunger for visible foot patrol can be at odds with the other demands placed on policing. The British appetite for foot patrol has been described as 'almost insatiable' (Morgan and Newburn, 1997, p160). The 2002/2003 British Crime Survey found that more than 50 per cent of respondents felt foot patrol should be among the top three priorities for the police (Wakefield, 2006). This is a long-standing disposition: in 1990, an Operational Police Review found that most people felt resources should be directed away from the reactive and crime-fighting role of the police and allocated instead to non-law-enforcement jobs such as foot patrol. Just 20 per cent of respondents believed that the police did a great deal or a fair amount of foot patrol (Police Federation of England and Wales and Police Superintendents' Association, 1990, p2). The Casey report listed visible, uniformed foot patrol as among the top five most important public priorities (Casey, 2008).

Media coverage of policing also inevitably tends to call for more foot patrol – but this iconic status of the 'bobby on the beat' means that it is difficult to explain to the public that the actual contribution of foot patrol to keeping them safe is more complex (Innes, 2004). Crawford and Lister (2006, p177) argue that this nostalgic yearning for local officers dealing with local problems is at times so strong that no attempt to replicate it can really measure up – the public will always be disappointed with the reality on the ground.

Nevertheless, the visibility of officers remains closely correlated with levels of confidence in the police (Police Foundation, 2022). The image of the bobby on the beat – the British police officer undertaking leisurely foot patrol, engaging with the community – is an enduring feature of the British policing landscape for cultural, political and symbolic reasons, and a powerful tool of police legitimation (Brunger, 2014). For the public, this visible, tangible, uniformed presence of the police can symbolise social inclusion and the active engagement of the state. However, this symbolic value is difficult to quantify. Particularly in times of austerity, therefore, it has been necessary for foot patrol to be justified in terms of its capacity to counter crime and disorder, to which this chapter turns next.

Foot patrol and crime

Foot patrol is often associated with preventing crime and reducing fear of crime. However, there is little evidence that random patrol alone can prevent crime (Kelling et al, 1974; Sherman and Eck, 2003; Telep and Weisburd, 2012). Notoriously, Clarke and Hough (1984) suggested that the likelihood of an officer on random foot patrol accidentally coming across a burglary in progress was about once every eight years.

On the other hand, there is a growing body of evidence that targeted foot patrol can affect crime levels (Sherman and Weisburd, 1995; Braga et al, 2012; Sorg et al, 2013). This form of foot patrol is known as hot spots policing. Hot spots policing is based on a single important insight about crime: that it isn't spread evenly, but is concentrated in particular places and times.

These 'hot spots' can be as small as a single street corner. Weisburd (2018) suggested that as much as 50 per cent of crime could be found in just 4 per cent of street segments. He based this on studies that had thrown up even greater concentrations: for example, Sherman et al (1989) found that 3.5 per cent of addresses in Minneapolis generated 50 per cent of all crime calls in a year; and Spelman (1995) found that 10 per cent of public places (such as schools and parks) generated 50 per cent of crime calls. Hot spots policing targets police resources at those concentrations of crime.

To undertake effective hot spots policing, forces need to first identify the locations where crime and disorder are most concentrated – their hot spots – and then focus law enforcement activity in these areas in order to act as a deterrent: 'map the crime and put the cops where the dots are' (Maple, 1999, quoted in Braga et al, 2019). The details of how these hot spots are identified and what activities should then be targeted are up to the force concerned; however, the vast majority of forces in the US use computer-assisted crime mapping, and have been doing so for some years (Braga et al, 2019).

The theory behind hot spots patrols is twofold: firstly that of deterrence – the likelihood of being caught and punished – and relatedly the reduction in opportunity to commit crime. These in turn are related to routine activity theory and rational choice theory – the idea that potential offenders will make rational decisions as to the benefit of particular forms of behaviour. Routine activity theory is distinctive in that it is not particularly interested in the sources of the offender's motivation. Instead, it focuses on the conditions that make crime possible: the convergence of a motivated offender, a suitable target or victim, and the absence of a capable guardian (Cohen and Felson, 1979). A motivated offender is someone willing to commit a crime and capable of doing so; a suitable target is one that has value to the offender; and guardianship is the presence of someone or something that is effective in deterring crime. Hot spots policing therefore seeks to increase the presence of capable guardians, and to deter motivated offenders from the particular area in which crime is concentrated.

Evidence has suggested that hot spots policing is effective, bringing small but significant reductions in crime and disorder. In a recent systematic review of hot spots policing research, nearly 80 per cent of studies generated significant benefits in terms of crime control (Braga et al, 2019). Moreover, there appears to be little displacement effect – where crime simply moves to another area. Indeed, Braga et al's review suggests that hot spots policing can instead have diffusion benefits – where more patrols in one area also appear to reduce crime in neighbouring areas.

However, while there is a lot of evidence about the efficacy of hot spots policing, there is some debate about how to undertake it. Firstly, determining hot spots is not entirely straightforward. For example, crime data can give police a good understanding of how many crimes are reported in a given area. However, mapping hot spots on crime alone may lead to a focus on high volume crimes at the expense of crimes that do more harm – though some studies suggest that recognising areas where high levels of low-level crime and disorder take place is still important for hot spots mapping (Harinam et al, 2022). It is also crucial for a confidence-based model of neighbourhood policing, where much of the crime and disorder which concerns local people will not register as high harm.

The shape and layout of cities may also matter. One study suggested that hot spots may not be as concentrated as suggested by Weisburd and others – and that concentrations may vary in different cities for reasons that are not fully understood (Hipp and Kim, 2017). If crime is concentrated in different ways in different cities, that has implications for how police forces should respond to it. A very tight focus on a few small areas may be less effective if crime in your city is more spread out. Crime may also vary more over time than has sometimes been suggested: crime may often look concentrated through random chance (Hipp and Kim, 2017). It is also important to consider what is being included and excluded in measures of crime – for example, measures of police recorded crime can be unreliable, particularly in areas with low confidence in the police or for crimes that are regularly under-reported, such as sex offences.

Once a hot spot has been identified, it also matters what police do with it. The frequency of hot spots patrols can make a significant difference to their effectiveness. One recent study suggested that even very small amounts of foot patrol could have an effect on serious violence; but that repeated patrols over several days for short amounts of time could have an even bigger effect (Bland et al, 2021).

Much of the early evidence on hot spots policing was based on law enforcement tactics (Braga, 2007). However, more recent studies have suggested that hot spots policing taking a more problem-oriented approach (see Chapter 6 for more on this), or effectively engaging the community, can have a greater effect than law enforcement approaches alone (Braga and Bond, 2008). One further question, to which this chapter returns later, is whether hot spots policing needs to be done by the police or whether non-police actors such as community wardens can be equally effective.

Overall, the weight of evidence suggests that targeted foot patrol does work. There are reductions in crime, which can sometimes be substantial; and rather than simply displacing crime, there appears to be a 'spillover' effect that sees crime also reduce in the areas surrounding those targeted. However, the evidence supporting a problem-oriented approach rather than a law enforcement one also touches on the reasons why foot patrol is so popular among the public. If foot patrol is to affect confidence as well as crime levels, it matters more what the police do, and the style in which they do it, than simply whether they are present (Hail et al, 2018).

Using targeted foot patrol to increase stop and searches, for example, is not likely to have a salutary effect on public confidence (Wood et al, 2014; Kochel and Weisburd, 2017). Instead, targeted foot patrol needs to be included as part of a wider strategy of visibility that recognises that the value of a police presence to the public is often only tangentially about their effectiveness in enforcing the law. People need to feel safe, and the presence of the police needs to be experienced as a reassuring one, not an added threat.

For this reason, the College of Policing has incorporated targeted foot patrol into its Neighbourhood Policing Guidelines (CoP, 2018a); but is clear that public perceptions, and identifying what different communities need, are a crucial part of the relevant information that needs to be incorporated into any effective plan to target police activity. Helping the public access the police, so that forces can understand what they need, is also a central part of visibility, and the element to which this chapter turns next.

Accessibility and familiarity

Accessibility and familiarity encompass a wide range of ideas, from how easy it is to report crimes to the police to whether residents know who their local officers are and how to contact them. In the report *Open all hours*, Povey (2001) described visibility, accessibility and familiarity as being vital to the work of reassuring the public.

Accessibility is defined as 'the ease with which the public can obtain appropriate police information, access services or make contact with staff' (Povey, 2001, p24). In Labour's 2004 White Paper, *Building communities, beating crime*, citizens were promised 'a more visible, accessible police presence on the streets and in their communities' (Home Office, 2004a, p8), and it formed a core part of the new NRPP and the Neighbourhood Policing Programme that followed. Accessing police services is undertaken in a range of different ways. These include the traditional ones such as visiting a police station or calling the police on 999 or 101, but can also include accessing a police force website, including by mobile phone; stopping an officer in the street; or directly contacting a local neighbourhood team at a meeting or by email or social media. Police-initiated communications through these means are discussed at greater length in the next chapter.

Familiarity is 'the extent to which police personnel both know and are known by the local community' (Povey, 2001, p24). From the earliest days of neighbourhood policing, it was recognised that visible but anonymous policing would not be sufficient to build the relationships and connections needed to support public confidence. The 2004 White Paper pledged that citizens should 'know who their local police officer, community support officer and wardens are – and who is in charge locally – and how they can be contacted' (Home Office, 2004a, p23). A 2006 progress report focused on familiarity and continuity as the key element of 'visible and accessible police': 'local people seeing and having regular contact with the same officers – week in and week out – who stay in the job long enough to build lasting and trusting relationships with the communities they serve' (Home Office, 2006). Visibility and familiarity were both regarded by the Association of Chief Police Officers as critical factors in the success of community engagement (ACPO, 2006, p15); familiarity in particular was seen as a factor in building trust.

Foot patrol

Officers in vehicles are visible, but as noted earlier in the chapter, there is debate as to whether they are accessible or reassuring. Singer (2004) found that officers, at least, believed that as patrol cars were highly visible they could offer a way of having a presence while officers did paperwork; and a report prepared by BMG Research for Her Majesty's Inspectorate for Constabulary and Fire and Rescue Services in 2018 suggested that a visible police presence in vehicles was nearly as important to the public as that presence on foot (BMG Research, 2019). However, the Audit Commission's (1996) study, *Streetwise*, found that respondents believed officers in cars were going to a crime that had already taken place, rather than being available to prevent crimes. Wilson and Kelling (1982) famously suggested that officers in cars used the vehicle as a barrier between themselves and residents.

The Povey report insisted that the quality of the visible presence mattered as well as the visibility itself, and quotes one Assistant Chief Constable as saying: 'a marked police vehicle with blue light and sirens activated sends a different message. This is currently visible policing, but we would suggest it is far from reassuring' (Povey, 2001, p23). This is supported by a recent study that found that patrol cars actually had a negative effect on citizens' feelings of safety (Borovec et al, 2019). Thus while patrol in vehicles can be beneficial to increasing the visibility of the police, it is not doing the same job as foot patrol in terms of presenting officers as approachable and accessible to residents in a neighbourhood, nor of reassuring them.

Foot patrol also increases officers' understanding of the areas they police in a way that is not available to those patrolling by car. This in turn allows officers to have a more textured understanding of who and what might threaten local order, understand the nature of problems and develop better relationships with communities (Peaslee, 2009; Colover and Quinton, 2018): 'One can only do good work by "being there" and getting to know the relationship between people and the spaces in which they live, work and play' (Wood et al, 2014). However, studies have suggested that this knowledge is rarely institutionalised; rather it is held by individual officers, making this knowledge fragile and easily lost through staff turnover (Lister et al, 2015). We return to the importance of local knowledge and continuity later in this section.

Police stations

Police stations were recognised by Povey as having a central role to play in reassurance: 'The police station, with its traditional blue lamp, is an enduring image of British policing that has almost as much symbolic importance as the uniformed bobby. In terms of public reassurance, it represents access to police services and, in emergency, a place of sanctuary' (Povey, 2001, p98, para 5.1).

The Audit Commission described the traditional police station as 'a tangible reminder of the police's presence, a source of reassurance second only to the sight of a "bobby on the beat"' (Audit Commission, 1996, p2). However, in the same report, it warned that much of the police estate was no longer fit for purpose and many stations needed to be closed. Some 700 stations had already been closed in the course of the 1990s (Rogers and Houston, 2004).

Over the next ten years, pressure on police forces to demonstrate efficiency saw the closure of more stations, especially in rural areas (Smith and Somerville, 2013), but also across major cities such as London (McLaughlin, 2008). Since 2010, this process has accelerated. A Freedom of Information request by the *Sunday Times* in September 2018 (Ungoed-Thomas et al, 2018) showed that 606 stations had closed since 2010; another Freedom of Information for LBC radio in November 2022 brought this number to 663 (Hand, 2022). Some 75 per cent of police stations open in London in 2010 had closed by 2022. The disappearance of police stations from many towns and cities has undoubtedly affected the capacity of the public to access police services.

The existence of police stations is a visible signifier of the presence of the police, as well as of their accessibility. Given their importance, it is surprising how little is known about the effect of the presence of police stations on public confidence (McLaughlin, 2008; Millie, 2012; Smith and Somerville, 2013). However, given what is known about what supports public confidence, it is hard to believe that the disappearance of such high-profile symbols of guardianship in communities has had no effect; and several studies have connected the disappearance of police stations with a sense among residents that the police are less present and responsive (Terpstra and Fyfe, 2015; O'Reilly et al, 2022).

Phoning the police

Another traditional route to contacting the police is to phone them. However, forces are increasingly overwhelmed by demand for their services. In particular, in the UK there is mounting evidence that the public has lost confidence in the 101 non-emergency number, as few forces are able to answer such calls within their target and other routes to access the police are unavailable (HMICFRS, 2020). In Somerset in 2018/2019, 43 per cent of 101 calls were unanswered. Other forces diverted 101 calls to answerphones, which might not be responded to for several days. Because of this, people increasingly phone 999 as a means of accessing the police, increasing demand on control rooms. The 2018 Public Perceptions of Policing report found there had been a decrease in the proportion of respondents who were confident that the police were easy to access or speak to in the event of an emergency – 63 per cent, down from 73 per cent the previous year (BMG Research, 2019).

Moreover, while the 101 system was set up to include other services, most of these withdrew due to lack of funding. This means that the police are also struggling with demand from those who actually need other services – making it harder for those who actually need the police to get through. Adding to this complexity from the point of view of public confidence is the suggestion that the general public do not necessarily distinguish between their faith in the police and in other services such as the local council (Jackson and Bradford, 2010). A lack of access to authorities in general could potentially therefore be reflected in drops in confidence in the police.

Online

In part as a result of this increasing pressure, many forces are trying to make it easier to report certain crimes online. For example, in areas such as Avon and Somerset, incidents like road collisions or shoplifting can be reported online and evidence uploaded. An increasing number of forces also encourage the online reporting of hate crimes. Some forces also allow the public to track the progress online of a crime they have reported (HMICFRS, 2020).

Forces have also begun to use social media to try to amplify their visible presence (Walsh and O'Connor, 2019). However, there is little evidence so far that social media can work in isolation to improve the visibility of the police rather than acting as a magnifier of a presence that is already there. The new Neighbourhood Policing Guidelines make reference to the need for more evidence on how social media can be used to improve visibility (CoP, 2018a). The use of social media for police-initiated community engagement is discussed in more detail in the next chapter.

Public meetings

Public meetings are generally regarded primarily as a means of the police engaging the community, and as part of the problem-solving process (see Chapters 4 and 5 for more on this). However, they also provide a means of increasing police accessibility and visibility; particularly in a context of police station closures and limited hours. In one study, respondents cited local ward panel meetings as one of the few venues where they could be sure of finding a police officer with whom they could have a face-to-face conversation (O'Reilly, 2020).

However, there are issues with the use of meetings as a means of increasing visibility and accessibility. One way of thinking about accessibility is as the extent to which the police are available to those who want their help, and the extent to which residents feel entitled to ask for that help (Marenin, 1998). This means that focusing on accessibility as a guiding principle can be dangerous if it means that officers concentrate on being responsive to everyone who approaches them, and only them. This is because the people that are most comfortable asking the police for help may not be the ones that need their help the most.

Some therefore instead argue that policing services should be allocated on the basis of need rather than demand. However, as seen in the last chapter, confidence in policing appears to rest on a broad engagement with the local community and an authentic response to issues raised by them. Moreover, in the signal crimes perspective, some residents were found to be much better at understanding and expressing the issues that mattered to the whole of the community than others. Accessibility through means such as public meetings should therefore be carefully managed to try to ensure that a range of voices are heard – but closing down these venues because the voices heard there may not be representative could be more damaging to public confidence than inequity of access.

Continuity

One crucial aspect of building familiarity, which in turn helps people feel comfortable in approaching police officers, is length in post. The Casey report (2008) noted that the public felt very strongly that they wanted to see more continuity, with officers and PCSOs serving a minimum of two years in their areas. In 2010, the Home Office promised to 'encourage forces to think creatively about ways to incentivise officers and PCSOs to stay in particular neighbourhoods' (Home Office, 2010b, p15).

Familiarity is a harder goal to achieve than visibility, as high staff turnover is a trickier problem to resolve than a lack of presence (Wakefield, 2007). Positive changes to how neighbourhood work is regarded within the force can ironically make continuity more difficult; Higgins (2018) describes how the increasing value of neighbourhood work to promotion had the perverse effect of encouraging officers to move on. In London, one officer described this regular changeover of officers as 'the Beast of the Met' (O'Reilly, 2020). Both turnover and abstractions (police being withdrawn for other duties) limit the level of familiarity that residents can develop with their local officers, and limit their capacity to become familiar with their areas and develop effective local knowledge (Crawford et al, 2003; Higgins, 2018). Staff turnover also creates a barrier to community policing initiatives involving partner organisations, which is explored further in Chapter 7.

However, there are also potential dangers in tying a designated officer to a particular area. The personal attributes of individual officers may become the deciding factor in the success of local policing; a situation exacerbated by the way neighbourhood policing entails a high level of autonomy and discretion (Crawford et al, 2003). While familiarity can allow officers to access local knowledge and enhance problem-solving, there is an 'ambiguity' to it, in that police who are attached to segments of the community may be unable to 'hold the required "detached stance"' (Crawford et al, 2003, p46).

There is also a risk that, in building close and cohesive community networks, some local residents are excluded. This is one of the reasons that Tilley (2008) argues for a form of 'weak' community policing, in which the police foster numerous weak ties (Granovetter, 1973) within and between communities and the police (Tilley, 2008, p46), rather than 'strong ties', which would entail closer and more personal but perhaps less inclusive relationships. These issues are explored further in Chapter 8. First, however, this chapter explores the possibility of bypassing some of these issues through bypassing the police themselves.

Plural policing

There are many more people involved in policing than just the police. While this plural policing is not wholly new – there have always been many different agents involved in 'social control' – it has proliferated in the UK due to successive government reforms in the last few decades. As Chapter 2 set out, the outcome of many of New Labour's reforms was to increase and coordinate the number of agencies involved in community safety. Local police officers, usually constables, were in effect to become coordinators (Savage, 2007b) of an extended policing family (Crawford et al, 2005) which would include PCSOs, local community wardens, volunteers, security guards and new local actors such as community safety managers (Hughes and Gilling, 2004; Robinson, 2006).

Police Community Support Officers

PCSOs were established by Section 38 of the Police Reform Act 2002. Their introduction was seen as a way of meeting the public's endless demand for foot patrol. The response to these new officers, whose powers were extremely limited compared to sworn constables, was initially sceptical on the part of both police officers and the public (Rogers, 2016).

However, PCSOs became valued for the way in which they could contribute to police visibility on the streets (O'Neill, 2015). A 2006 Home Office assessment found PCSOs spent up to 70 per cent of their time on patrol (Cooper et al, 2006) – by contrast to an earlier PA Consulting report (PA Consulting Group, 2001), which had found that police constables were spending just 17 per cent of their time on the beat. The assessment also found that the public valued the role and PCSOs were seen as being more approachable and recognisable than regular police officers (Cooper et al, 2006). Their very lack of authority contributed to the guardianship role of police patrols, facilitating rapport and familiarity and encouraging other agencies and residents to step up where they might have left a warranted officer with greater powers to deal with a problem alone (Paskell, 2007).

Much of the success of PCSOs has been ascribed to the tendency for them to spend long periods of time working in a single area, not least as they are rarely subjected to abstraction. For example, Loveday and Smith (2015) cite an inspector in London: 'Some of my PCSOs have worked their patch for more than 8 years now. My longest serving PCs can boast less than a quarter of this time on the locality.' PCSOs were said to take pride in the volume of intelligence reports they were able to file on known offenders in the area, a volume that simply could not have been generated without substantial and long-term local knowledge (Loveday and Smith, 2015).

However, there was less evidence that PCSOs had a substantive effect on reducing crime and anti-social behaviour (Sutherland, 2014), which became of increasing concern after 2010 with budget pressures and the end of ring-fenced funding in 2014. This meant that PCSOs had to be considered in the round of police expenditure, with the opportunity cost of employing full officers instead – and in a context where, unlike warranted officers, PCSOs could be subject to compulsory severance (Loveday and Smith, 2015).

Neighbourhood wardens

The New Labour government also oversaw a parallel growth in other types of patrol officers. In 2000, the government launched its neighbourhood wardens scheme (in residential areas), managed through local councils, and street wardens (aimed at providing highly visible uniformed patrol) a year after. Within two years, there were nearly 1,500 wardens funded by central government and spread across the country (Crawford and Lister, 2004).

The benefits of the lack of authority that were found with PCSOs also appeared to stretch to this wider 'policing family'. Residents were more willing to give information about crime and disorder to street wardens than to the police, and again, precisely because of their lack of legal powers, '[t]hey were given information because they provided a visible, uniformed, neutral and sympathetic presence on the street' (Johnston, 2003, p194).

One particular advantage of neighbourhood wardens is that they are able to provide an effective long-term presence and support, and to tap in directly to local authority resources (Crawford et al, 2005). These are of course available to police officers and PCSOs, but at one remove, and successful use of these may be dependent on building up effective partnership relationships over time (see Chapter 7 for more on this). However, local authorities have been subject to even greater financial pressures than the police, and many councils have had to withdraw or limit these roles.

Reception

While the growth of plural policing undoubtedly contributed to an increase in visible guardianship in neighbourhoods, this growth initially faced substantial criticism. The introduction of PCSOs was fiercely resisted by the Police Federation, which saw it as policing on the cheap (Rogers, 2016). The lack of powers that make PCSOs more approachable also means that they often can do little to address poor behaviour other than to negotiate or to call on warranted officers. From a pragmatic perspective, some officers initially believed that PCSOs simply made more work for the police (Johnston, 2007).

Others expressed concern from the perspective of the democratic governance of such a multiplicity of different actors (Rhodes, 1997; Loader, 2000). For example, the lack of regulation that encouraged pluralisation through allowing a more visible presence for less money also meant much less oversight of the activities and behaviour of the new plural actors. While PCSOs and neighbourhood wardens are governed by the force and the local authority respectively, this is not the case for others operating in this space. To whom should a private security guard in a privately owned shopping centre be accountable, given its nature as a public space? Other issues around pluralisation include information sharing (Johnston, 2003) and coordination of activities (Robinson, 2006).

And as with foot patrol by warranted officers, the way that PCSOs and others behave while on patrol also matters to confidence; a visible presence alone is not sufficient. If PCSOs are persistently used for crime control purposes, as Cosgrove and Ramshaw (2015) noted, then the benefits of their position as a bridge between the community and the police could be wasted.

Nevertheless, the merit of PCSOs in particular has been widely recognised, with most forces retaining their services. Subsequent research has suggested that hot spots patrols can be undertaken by PCSOs just as effectively as warranted officers (Ariel et al, 2016), underlining the value of the role to the neighbourhood policing model. As one internal review put it: 'the value that PCSOs generate through high-visibility patrol, partnership working, tackling ASB and freeing up officer hours is beyond doubt' (Sutherland, 2014, p81).

These findings tally with the underlying mechanisms of confidence explored in Chapter 3. It is likely the presence of a visible symbol of social control and guardianship that supports public confidence, rather than the capacity of these agents to make arrests and enforce the law. Forces should therefore regard PCSOs and neighbourhood wardens in particular as potentially effective resources that can help manage demand on the police, and support public confidence in the authorities as a whole.

Summary

The need for an effective, relationship-building presence in communities is recognised by the College of Policing in its *Neighbourhood policing practice guidelines*. It underlines that 'there is a need to ensure sufficient capacity, capability and continuity of resource ... to enable productive and trusting relationships with communities and partners to be maintained' (CoP, 2018a, np).

Despite this, visible, accessible and familiar policing is an element of neighbourhood policing under increasing threat, both from the current trajectory of policing and from wider societal changes. An increased focus on vulnerability and hidden harms leads to police resources being focused on crimes taking place behind closed doors. Budget pressures have caused the closure of police stations, meaning that swathes of towns and cities have no consistent police presence. And forces have focused on how resources can be allocated towards the greatest risk and harm, undermining the justification for foot patrol in areas of low immediate risk. Yet those are the places where people live.

Visibility is mediated by the environment, including the architecture of an area; but also by the social context. Volume crimes have reduced, as young people most at risk of engaging in anti-social behaviour live increasingly indoor lives; and the entry-level criminal behaviour of earlier decades, such as car theft, becomes the arena of sophisticated criminal gangs, or an activity that takes place behind closed doors.

However, these changes to crime and demand have yet to blunt the public appetite for visible guardianship. Public perceptions of levels of foot patrol are closely linked to their confidence in the police as a whole – in part because the presence of the police symbolises the engagement of the authorities in protecting local order, and by extension, recognising that these neighbourhoods and their residents have value and are worthy of protection.

While visibility is crucial to confidence, it has a limited effect on both confidence and crime levels by itself. Targeted foot patrol has a recognised effect on reducing crime and disorder at hot spots, and patrol can therefore be an effective way of tackling problem areas. However, the effect of what the police do is mediated by the style in which they do it: a law enforcement approach is less effective than one that incorporates a concern for what the local community want and how they want it done. If targeted foot patrol is aggressive, or damages trust, then the benefits of effectiveness in crime reduction may be outweighed by the costs in legitimacy and confidence.

Visibility in the context of neighbourhood policing is about more than just what can be seen. It is much more effective in supporting confidence if combined with the kinds of activity that see local police getting to know an area and its residents, and are seen to be listening and responding to them. Indeed, highly visible policing can sometimes be actively damaging to the work of neighbourhood officers, if it is overbearing, focused on enforcement or otherwise undertaken in a way that damages relationships.

Visibility instead needs to be seen as a mechanism with a purpose: to increase confidence, through familiarity, accessibility and reassuring the public that the task of ensuring local order has been assumed by the authorities. An effective and visible presence in communities therefore requires a long-term commitment on the part of police organisations and a recognition that a visible presence is a necessary step, but only the first step, to building the long-term relationships on which public confidence and police legitimacy thrive.

Questions for further consideration

1. Under what circumstances might hot spots policing be a poor strategy to implement as part of a neighbourhood or community policing model?
2. How can the lessons of police visibility outlined in this chapter be translated to large rural jurisdictions?

Further reading

Braga, A.A., Turchan, B.S., Papachristos, A.V. and Hureau, D.M. 2019. Hot spots policing and crime reduction: An update of an ongoing systematic review and meta-analysis. *Journal of Experimental Criminology*, 15(3): 289–311.

College of Policing. 2018c. *Neighbourhood policing guidelines: Supporting material for frontline officers, staff and volunteers*. Coventry: College of Policing.

Rogers, C. 2016. *Plural policing: Theory and practice*. Bristol: Policy Press.

Wakefield, A. 2006. *The value of foot patrol: A review of research*. London: Police Foundation.

5

Engaging communities

Introduction

'A key criticism of police approaches to consultation previously is that it has been constructed within a mindset that sees its primary purpose as educating a misinformed public about the realities of policing' (Jones and Newburn, 2001, p50). As this quote suggests, police forces want the public to understand their jobs better. However, it is the job of neighbourhood teams to understand communities better. Community engagement was one of the three core 'mechanisms' by which neighbourhood policing was expected to deliver improvements in public perceptions and confidence in the police. The Labour government's policy agenda prioritised the involvement of the public in the delivery of public services in general. It believed that the engagement of the public in policing had both instrumental benefits to the police, but also to communities in terms of capacity-building.

Nearly 20 years on from the original Neighbourhood Policing Programme, the necessity of community engagement is embedded in policy and College of Policing (CoP) guidance, but practice at neighbourhood level is variable. Officers struggle with resource limitations, a changing media landscape, and an often risk-averse organisational culture.

This chapter sets out the benefits of community engagement and what is known about particular methods of engaging. It begins with a discussion of the context of community engagement; the legislative requirements and the current status of guidance and training in this area, given the uncertain future of the Police Education Qualifications Framework (PEQF) and its limited reach to serving officers.

It then offers some frameworks for understanding police–community engagement. This begins with a discussion of the purposes of community engagement, and the need for officers to be clear and transparent as to why they are engaging in the first place. It discusses some different typologies for community engagement, and why some of these are more useful and others, given the restrictions within which the police operate.

The chapter then discusses the strengths and weaknesses of public meetings as a way of engaging with the public, and offers some suggestions as to how meetings can be organised and run in a way that supports the work of neighbourhood officers. Effective meetings in turn can allow resources to be diverted to other means of engagement beyond the public meeting, such as outreach or environmental visual audits.

Finally, the chapter looks at communications in neighbourhood policing – from the benefits of more traditional approaches such as printed newsletters and newspaper stories, to the pros and cons of engaging on social media. The chapter concludes with a reminder of the importance of purpose: community engagement in neighbourhood policing is not about educating the public. Instead, it needs to be authentic, grounded in the community, and two-way – understanding what residents need and building those relationships – to support public confidence in the police.

Community engagement in context

Effective police–community engagement has officially been recognised as central to confidence and legitimacy since the 1980s. Since then it has been embedded into legislation and guidance. This chapter begins by looking at the requirements set out in legislation to engage with the public before examining how engagement is articulated in the guidance provided by the College of Policing.

The Scarman report, which followed the Brixton riots of 1981, warned that the police had become disengaged from the public. The subsequent Police and Criminal Evidence Act of 1984 was the first to set out a legal requirement to consult the public in order to get their views on policing and to encourage public co-operation with the police. The arrangements made by forces were generally open public meetings chaired by a member of the local police authority, often known as Police and Community Consultation Groups (PCCGs). The was consolidated under the Police Act of 1996.

However, the PCCGs suffered from numerous problems, discussed at greater length later in this chapter. Firstly, the police authority members who were chairing the meetings were intended to be independent. However, they were often regarded as having been 'captured' by the police and were rarely confrontational. The meetings were dominated by the police and their agenda, and were widely acknowledged as failing to work as intended to improve police–public relations (Morgan and Maggs, 1985; Elliott and Nicholls, 1996). Instead, they became forums in which the police sought to legitimate decisions already made (Bullock, 2014).

The principle of engagement was nevertheless acknowledged as crucial to building working relationships between forces and the public. As discussed in Chapter 2, the Labour government made it a major part of policy across the public sector to enshrine community engagement in policy and practice, and to do so at a local level as much as at a strategic one.

The Crime and Disorder Act 1998 set out a requirement for local councils and the police to carry out an audit of local crime and disorder problems and to consult on the basis of this audit. Guidance was given with regard to three groups: 'specified bodies' (which could include groups such as youth organisations, the Racial Equality Council and 'organised gay and lesbian groups'); the general public; and 'significant hard-to-reach groups, where no adequate representative organisation exists' (Hough and Tilley, 1998). Forces were enjoined to take a 'fresh and critical look' (Hough and Tilley, 1998, p28) at existing consultative arrangements to ensure that they were fit for purpose, and to consider new consultation methods such as commissioning focus groups or holding public meetings in gay bars. The Local Government Act 1999 built on this, putting a duty on police authorities – which were partly made of up councillors and officially fell under the responsibility of local councils – to achieve 'Best Value' in the provision of services to the public and therefore to consult on the planning and delivery of police services.

Other legislation and guidance during this time included the Race Relations (Amendment) Act 2000, which gave police authorities a duty to consult on the impact of any policies on racial equality; the institution of Crime and Disorder Reduction Partnerships which came into operation in 1999; and the second National Policing Plan published in 2002, which underlined the importance of police authorities and forces engaging with the public to inform priorities and to set targets.

By the time that the third National Policing Plan was published in 2004, the focus of New Labour's priorities was firmly on citizen engagement, and a major plank of reforms was 'citizen-focused policing' (Home Office, 2004a). This entailed five major strands, including neighbourhood policing (which itself involved considerable public engagement); 'effective engagement with the public'; and a promise that citizens would have a 'real say' in how they were policed, as well as promising a statutory minimum requirement for forces to provide information on local policing. The White Paper *Building communities, beating crime* laid out in comprehensive detail the expectations on the police, including 'a requirement on the police and other agencies to work directly with local people to identify the problems that are most important to them' (Home Office, 2004a, p24). By the time of the publication of the 2008 White Paper, *From the neighbourhood to the national*, community engagement was entrenched as one of the central planks of neighbourhood policing; though in the wake of that year's Casey Review, further pledges were made, including joint community engagement efforts between the police and local authorities.

Following the 2010 change of government, and the establishment of Police and Crime Commissioners (PCCs) in 2011, the requirements to consult and engage with the public remained; though the ideological motivation behind these shifted. There remains a legislative responsibility on the part of PCCs to consult. The Police Reform and Social Responsibility Act 2011 replaced the previous 'tripartite' system of police accountability. PCCs' responsibilities according to the Act are to '(a) secure the maintenance of the police force for that area, and (b) secure that the police force is efficient and effective' (Section 1(6)) by holding the Chief Constable accountable. This responsibility extends to ensuring the efficiency and effectiveness of the Chief Constable's engagement with local people. The Act also insists PCCs have to consult the public before issuing a Police and Crime Plan, and with regard to the precept (the amount collected through Council Tax that goes towards local policing). As discussed earlier, this reflects the move towards democratisation as an expression of accountability and away from public confidence as a target.

This legal framework post-2010 is therefore focused on strategic consultation and priorities, rather than the local, confidence-rooted focus of the previous administration. There does remain a requirement on forces to consult at a local level: Section 34 of the Police Reform and Social Responsibility Act 2011 requires forces to supply information and seek the views of the public about crime and disorder in their neighbourhood and hold regular public meetings in every neighbourhood. However, it is striking in this context that the government White Paper of 2021, the *Beating crime plan*, contains no mention of police–community engagement or consultation as to neighbourhood priorities: these are instead to be 'data-driven'.

Given the absence of explicit Home Office support for confidence as a metric, and its limited support for community engagement as a local mechanism, the institutionalisation of community engagement as part of police practice at a neighbourhood level is noteworthy. This can in part be ascribed to the CoP and its remit to base police practice and standards on knowledge and evidence; but also to the persistence of patterns of practice in neighbourhood policing, despite the extent to which it has become fractured on a national level (Higgins, 2018).

This has taken a while to be fully developed. Much of the guidance provided by the CoP in its Authorised Professional Practice page on community engagement (CoP, 2013) is less around how to engage with the community and more about understanding the community to be engaged with. Thus considerable advice is given as to drawing up a neighbourhood profile and community impact assessment – but almost no guidance is offered as to how to actually engage, other than to devolve decisions to neighbourhood officers (CoP, 2013).

More recent guidance has improved on this. The Neighbourhood Policing Guidelines issued in 2018 encourage officers to find out how communities want to be engaged with, and to consider the barriers to engagement. They also offer practical advice on the benefits of different types of information provision and list a range of different proactive methods of engagement beyond beat meetings and neighbourhood surgeries. The Guidelines encourage officers to tailor methods to the needs of communities and to encourage communities to become involved in the engagement process itself, for example, through chairing local meetings. The Guidelines are particularly useful in terms of setting policing priorities.

More comprehensive guidance on community engagement was provided through the curriculum of the PEQF, designed to facilitate three new entry routes to policing, ensuring that all new police officers are qualified to degree level. Community policing is presented as having four key aspects – targeted foot patrol, community engagement, problem-solving and crime prevention – and learners are explicitly expected to understand the strengths and weaknesses of different methods of engagement.

The extent to which PEQF learning will be institutionalised within the police service is still unclear, and delivery of the curriculum can vary significantly between university providers. The substantial integration of community engagement into the curriculum suggests a broader institutionalisation of the need for engagement, and knowledge of best practice, than the limited Authorised Professional Practice suggests. However, the curriculum is not on offer to serving officers, and ongoing professional development in these areas is limited. Moreover, with the announcement in November 2022 that degree entry routes will after all not be mandatory for new entrants (Braverman, 2022), it is not clear at the time of writing whether this curriculum will be offered to all new officers. As such, while the need for community engagement is clearly recognised within the College, the cascading of best practice is still fragmentary.

This means that despite broad support for and understanding of the need for enhanced police–public engagement there remains a risk that community engagement becomes unmoored. Specifically, without central pressure, the more difficult, resource-heavy and sometimes exasperating forms of community engagement may be exchanged for what is easy, superficially effective, and tells the police what they want to hear. The next section offers a framework for understanding different types of community engagement, and what they can achieve for forces.

Frameworks of engagement

In order to effectively engage with the community, police need to understand why they are doing so, and what kind of engagement would best suit that purpose. There are a number of typologies that have been developed to understand the different kinds of community engagement, and this section explores some of the ways that these have been adapted to policing.

Purposes of engagement

It is not always clear to forces what the purpose of their consultation or engagement actually is (Jones and Newburn, 2001), and sometimes officers end up paying lip service to the idea, or engaging so ineffectively that any benefits are lost. Recognising this, the CoP's Neighbourhood Policing Guidelines warn that it is important 'to be clear and open about why you want to engage and are using particular engagement methods' (CoP, 2018c). Potential purposes listed by the CoP include building trust after a critical incident, being more responsive to residents' needs, and encouraging communities to take ownership of local problems.

This is particularly important if the aims of the police do not marry with the expectations of the communities being engaged with. For example, residents may believe that the main purpose of taking part in an engagement event is to gain more access to police resources and to encourage police action on specific problems (Jones and Newburn, 2001). If the police are focused on handing problems over to the community, or simply being seen to be consulting, the outcome of the event will be effective for neither party.

A second consideration is the level at which engagement takes place. One way of understanding these distinctions is Myhill's (2006) typology, used by the CoP's Authorised Professional Practice. It sets out three levels – democratic mandate, intermediate strategic and neighbourhood policing – each of which is tied to a separate purpose. The purposes of engagement at the 'democratic mandate' level are accountability and legitimacy, setting the 'dominant philosophy' of policing. It is not entirely clear whether this level is envisaged as being national or at PCC level, but it is clearly a strategic level of engagement. Intermediate strategic level includes engagement in policy and planning, as well as critical incidents, to influence strategic priorities and decisions, including around equalities analysis (CoP, 2013). The final level is neighbourhood policing, involving local people in decisions about the issues that most concern them, and setting local priorities.

One important point to draw from this is the importance of distinguishing between force-level accountability and community participation in local policing. Problems can emerge if participants are unclear, or not in agreement, about the purpose of the forum itself. This was a perennial problem in the Scarman-era PCCGs; forces wanted to talk about strategic level issues but community participants wanted to talk about local problems in their neighbourhoods. If residents wanting to discuss local issues feel that these concerns are not being heard, the engagement process can actually damage public confidence in policing.

Local councillors, in particular, can find it hard to resist using such forums to make political points (O'Reilly, 2020). Where relationships are poor this can reach extremes: one case study mentioned by Jones and Newburn (2001) observed that the official Labour Group on Bristol City Council had a policy of non-contact with the police. In order to resolve this, senior officers were forced to 'gatecrash' meetings of local agencies and organisations. More commonly, it may be difficult for partners such as councillors involved at multiple levels of police engagement to make distinctions between the purpose of particular events, and so it is important that officers make this clear and transparent from the beginning of each encounter.

Types of engagement

Myhill's (2006) framework is drawn in part from existing typologies of community engagement but adapted to policing. The bottom level of engagement is information and reassurance: promising to make balanced and objective information available at a local level, through a range of information channels. Forces are often very comfortable with this level of engagement; indeed, much scholarship warns that police tend to default to 'broadcast' modes rather than two-way engagement. Communications strategies through traditional and social media are explored further later in the chapter.

The second level is monitoring and accountability. This is about forces being transparent and accountable, and includes means such as Independent Advisory Groups and citizen monitoring of police complaints. The third level is strategic consultation: keeping the public informed, adopting their priorities at a strategic level where possible and providing feedback, through a range of consultation methods. These two levels might fit quite closely with the remit of PCCs as described in the last section, which were only in their infancy when Myhill's review was (re)published.

The fourth level is partnership and co-operation; here defined as using the 'help, advice and expertise [of the public] to the maximum possible extent' (Myhill, 2006, p18). This incorporates local action meetings, the Special Constabulary and volunteering. The final and top level of community engagement in Myhill's typology is empowerment. The promise to citizens here is that 'you can take the final decision unless there is a clear justification preventing this'. This level of engagement is described as public-initiated, police-supported problem-solving initiatives.

There are some issues with this typology, and in particular with the final two levels. For example, it is not clear that Special Constables are significantly more reflective of the communities they serve, given that for younger volunteers in particular, service is often seen as a route into the police (Pepper, 2014; Callender et al, 2020). It is also notable that the partnership and co-operation level still envisages partners co-operating with the police rather than the other way around. However, this is still perhaps a more realistic level of engagement than the final level, of empowerment. It is not clear that the police 'form', the unavoidable structure of the police–public relationship, always allows the transparency and ceding of power that authentic empowerment would require (Harkin, 2015).

Perhaps a more useful metaphor is to think of engagement as a three-stage process, with democratic accountability at the top, the remit of national politics and PCCs, and force-level operational strategy at the second level. The purpose of these two levels is to consult, to gather public views and to hold the police democratically accountable. There are a limited number of potential outputs, which are predetermined by PCCs and forces before consulting, and how the results of engagement are used is up to those consulting. This is essentially a one-way process in which the community is engaged with in order to feed in its views; these are incorporated into internal thinking in a process that is, like sausage-making, thankfully hidden from view; and from which policy and strategy emerge.

At ground level, however, is the third part of the process, the one most relevant to public confidence and to neighbourhood policing. This is where police need to embed themselves deep into the community through multiple different means. Information and broadcasting can by all means be used for reassurance at this level – if confidence is thought of as a garden to be cultivated, this is watering the grass – but if it is to be effective it has to be grounded in authentic engagement, explored in more depth later in the chapter. Some of the efforts here will be formal public meetings which, for all their faults (discussed next), allow authentic contact between police and public. Others may be more innovative, high-resource initiatives. There is potential for authentic partnerships and even co-production at this level, but the real limits of this should be acknowledged, again as early and transparently as possible. Nothing at this level should be purely one-way.

While engagement and consultation at higher levels may be more high profile, and give the impression of having more importance, there is little evidence of its effects on confidence and legitimacy – which are often most affected, as seen in Chapter 3, on the real encounters that residents have with the police and the beliefs that they hold about them. Moreover, strategic consultation cannot identify at a neighbourhood level the issues that residents are genuinely concerned by – the signals to which the police need to respond to effectively build confidence and legitimacy. It is neighbourhood-level community engagement that does that, and the rest of this chapter explores some of the key means of doing so effectively.

The persistence of the public meeting

The public meeting has a poor reputation. The CoP's Neighbourhood Policing Guidelines acknowledge that meetings can be effective ways of engaging the community, but warns that they can suffer from poor representativeness and low attendance levels, and suggests that alternative methods can reach a broader cross-section (CoP, 2018c). Poorly run meetings can lead to the wrong local priorities being adopted – for example, to pay lip service to community concerns even when police know they can do little to address an issue (Foster and Jones, 2010). Police can overrule residents, relying on their own estimation of harm and risk rather than those of community participants (Bullock and Leeney, 2013).

Such concerns are not new. Three years after the Scarman report established PCCGs, a Home Office study confirmed that most forces had implemented them. Whether participants' hearts were in it was a different matter. 'More prevalent is the view that in many parts of the country they are probably a waste of time, but that in the meantime, everyone has to go through the motions' (Morgan and Maggs, 1985, p14). By the end of the decade, there was a consensus that consultation through PCCGs was not working as intended (Elliott and Nicholls, 1996).

Instead of incorporating residents' views on strategic issues such as the Policing Plan, the meetings were simply legitimating the status quo. The structure of the meetings may have affected this. Police-appointed chairs may have contributed to the committees becoming self-selecting groups of supportive local organisational representatives (Bull and Stratta, 1994, p245). Officers tended to monitor and control what made its way onto the agenda, which, in turn, were often dominated by operational police issues (Myhill et al, 2003). In effect, meetings were used to 'broadcast information and to rubber stamp decisions that had already been made' (Bullock, 2018, pp246–247). Nevertheless, around 75 per cent of police authorities still ran these sorts of meetings (Myhill et al, 2003).

However, the most repeated critiques of meetings as a venue for police–public engagement are low participation and poor representativeness of communities, as noted in the CoP guidelines. Attendance at police–public consultative meetings is often low (Myhill et al, 2003; Harkin, 2014; Higgins, 2018). The post-Scarman PCCG meetings often had fewer than 15 members of the public, and they were sometimes outnumbered by officials. Those who did attend were overwhelmingly White and over the age of 40 (Elliott and Nicholls, 1996). Low attendance may not just be an outcome of public apathy, but can contribute to it (Harfield, 1997); the Home Office in 2010 acknowledged that, after nearly a decade of community engagement as part of neighbourhood policing, the common image of local meetings remained 'the same few people sitting around in a local hall' (Home Office, 2010a, p15, para 2.29).

The factors affecting attendance are complex. In some areas, only meetings addressing issues of immediate local concern attract a large turnout (Myhill et al, 2003); ordinary day-to-day considerations attracted much less engagement. Some, including the CoP, have suggested tensions between police and ethnic minorities, or the lack of existing community networks, can lead to low attendance (Grinc, 1994; Skogan et al, 1999). However, participation is not always skewed towards wealthier communities. Some studies have found attendance rates to be higher in areas with poor housing and high crime rates (Bullock and Sindall, 2014): 'beat meetings give people a place to go to do something about them' (Skogan and Steiner, 2004, pii).

Low attendance can sometimes become an issue for the legitimacy of public meetings if these are not representative. Studies found the post-Scarman PCCGs to be dominated by White, middle-class, older citizens, who didn't always reflect the communities they were meant to represent (Bull and Stratta, 1994; Myhill et al, 2003). More generally, being active in community groups is often associated with being well-educated, relatively wealthy and possessing social capital, which is discussed further in Chapter 8 (Herbert, 2006). Some have suggested that the dominance of these more middle-class citizens can itself put others off from joining in (Harfield, 1997).

However, concerns about representativeness are sometimes felt more strongly by police officers than citizens themselves: in one study, officers used the unrepresentativeness of some neighbourhood ward panels to justify the police overriding their decisions on local policing priorities. However, residents engaged with the panels were much less concerned: 'they're representative of people who are interested' (O'Reilly, 2020).

The question of representation is a crucial one in the context of neighbourhood policing, and one raised elsewhere in this book. The signal crime perspective suggests that there is often broad agreement among residents in a given area about what the local problems are; but that this varies greatly between areas. Moreover, it suggests that some individuals who are highly engaged in their local areas may have a much better idea of the kind of problems that matter to communities than those who are less engaged (Innes, 2005b). In order to find out about local problems, therefore, officers might therefore do much better to focus on certain key individuals then expend time on gathering the opinions of those who are less involved with their own communities – a suggestion explored further in the next section.

However, different types of crime and disorder may still affect different residents in different ways. Good community engagement therefore needs to understand these differences and connect with communities beyond those most engaged. This is particularly the case if some communities within a locality are not represented through existing forums or networks.

A lack of representativeness can also bring other problems; particularly when community engagement is undertaken with a view to decision-making, for example, on local priorities. There are risks that decisions taken by a small number of active citizens may not represent the wider population, and will leave those who are not active participants feeling ignored and resentful (Herbert, 2006; Foster and Jones, 2010; Bullock and Leeney, 2013). A lack of representativeness also risks a dominant group being able to direct police action against a minority group with which they have an issue (Harfield, 1997). Public meetings can therefore be dangerous if forces rely entirely upon them for community engagement purposes.

Nevertheless, there are good reasons for the endurance of public meetings as a means for police–public engagement. Firstly, they are not particularly expensive. Neighbourhood meetings are usually scheduled for a handful of times a year and take up no more than a few hours of neighbourhood officers' time. This is a considerably lower investment of resources and time than most of the alternatives (to which the chapter turns next) – so long as the meetings are effective.

Public meetings allow issues to be explored in discussion, which can operate as a mechanism for the public to let off steam, to hold officers to account, to build personal relationships, and to assist with intelligence gathering (Myhill et al, 2003). Meetings play a function as somewhere that people can 'vent' and be heard, contributing to the 'voice' element of procedural justice. They also, as noted in the last chapter, enhance the accessibility of the police and the authorities in general, particularly in circumstances where local police stations have closed, and where even local council offices may be out of reach. Meetings also allow for informal conversations before and after the meetings themselves. This face-to-face contact can facilitate trust and accountability for participants (O'Reilly, 2020).

The potential for all of these functions means that meetings have value even when attendance is low; the structure is in place should there be an issue for which a resident feels attendance is justified. When things are going smoothly, policing is 'socially invisible' (Reiner, 2010, p64) and citizens may have little interest in participating in forums set up to discuss it. In short, they might not always want to go to a police–public meeting, but when they do, they need them to be there: 'it's still important that people see that there is a procedure for them to be empowered and given a voice' (O'Reilly, 2020). Attendance and participation can thus be seen as both input and output, part of an ongoing process of negotiation of legitimacy and confidence.

However, the meetings need to be well-structured and preferably not run by the police. Good practice could include ensuring that meetings have a chair drawn from the local community who can reach out beyond the relationships which officers already have. 'Ward panels' of local residents, such as those set up in London, with a core of local residents and meetings open to the wider public, have the capacity to establish continuity in community contacts that can support the work of neighbourhood officers, while alleviating some of the demand on them (O'Reilly, 2020).

The persistence of public meetings is therefore less of a mystery than their well-known faults might suggest. They have real value to neighbourhood police officers in terms of trust and confidence as well as building local knowledge and gathering intelligence. However, the flaws outlined here also mean that going beyond the meeting is necessary for effective and representative engagement.

Beyond the public meeting

The well-recorded problems with public meetings as a form of engagement have led to regular exhortations to forces to try other methods of engaging with the public. The 2004 White Paper called for 'direct and continuous engagement' between the police and the public: 'Moving beyond relying on public meetings as a sole form of engagement is a key aim of our reforms' (Home Office, 2004a, p63, para 3.45). Yet, four years on, at the culmination of the roll-out of the national Neighbourhood Policing Programme, the Casey report found that 74 per cent of forces appeared to still be relying on them (Casey, 2008).

The Flanagan review of that year again called for public meetings to be 'supplemented by more innovative engagement methods that increase representation' (Flanagan, 2008, p66). But there was little in the White Paper or the Flanagan review by way of concrete examples of these other activities, other than a nod to the street briefings and door knocking that had been successful in the pilot of the National Reassurance Policing Programme (NRPP), and to which the chapter returns shortly. Her Majesty's Inspectorate of Constabulary (HMIC, 2008) found that effective community engagement went beyond scheduled meetings, but it did not explain the distinction between a 'traditional' meeting and 'innovations' such as Police and Community Together meetings or Neighbourhood Watch. National Policing Improvement Agency guidance suggests that neighbourhood engagement should go beyond public meetings, but not that it should leave them behind (NPIA, 2010, p25). No government guidance suggested that forces abandon meetings; and as noted in the last chapter, neighbourhood meetings are now a legal requirement.

Instead, forces have been encouraged to widen the range of activities that they use to engage communities. There is sound evidence to support this, beyond the limitations of meetings that has already been addressed. The most successful public engagement seems to be that which is flexible and adapted to particular communities (Pate et al, 1986). The evaluation of the NRPP noted that traditional public meetings by themselves did not appear to change perceptions of police engagement. The trial sites that did see significant improvements in perceptions of engagement had undertaken activities other than meetings, including ' "open forum" events, large scale public surveys, the use of outreach workers, door knocking exercises and dedicated media officers to ensure wide press coverage of reassurance initiatives' (Tuffin et al, 2006, p86). One site's early 'open forum' saw residents using flags to identify problem areas on a scale model of the neighbourhood (Tuffin et al, 2006, p86). However, it is not clear which of these activities might have had the most influence on perceptions.

A variety of alternative methods of community engagement have been explored. The CoP's Neighbourhood Policing Guidelines suggest that officers consider street briefing, door knocking, surveys and using outreach workers (CoP, 2018c). Door knocking seems to be effective in crime reduction (Myhill, 2006). Community engagement has been enhanced in some forces by focus groups, particularly for vulnerable and hard-to-reach groups. Environmental visual audits, involving officers and relevant partners reviewing a local area on foot alongside residents, have been used effectively in many areas (Turley et al, 2012).

'Outreach' work undertaken by forces appears to be successful, and is a particularly effective way of targeting hard-to-reach groups; though in practice it has often been found to be more concerned with profile-raising than interactive consultation (Myhill et al, 2003). The quality and effectiveness of outreach may also rest on who the police reach out to. A tendency to rely on existing, well-established groups can mean that less easy to reach groups are largely left disengaged (Lister et al, 2015). On the other hand, using existing networks of community groups can make the process of engagement easier and more effective (Bullock and Leeney, 2013).

This ambiguity underlines the need for officers to spend time thinking about the community or communities that they are engaging with, and who they need to hear from. The CoP advises that all forces should carry out a community mapping exercise, paying particular attention to groups that may be more affected both by Stop and Search and the types of crime targeted by Stop and Search, as legitimacy may be of particular concern in these communities (CoP, 2018c). This contributes to the capacity of forces to adapt their community engagement activity to the needs and preferences of different communities.

The early signal crimes work that underpinned the NRPP suggested the use of structured interviews with 'key individuals', who were defined as those residents who had particular knowledge and experience of local problems. These might be people who are more present in public spaces, or who are more embedded in local networks (Innes, 2005b). For example, a resident who commutes to a different city most days may have less understanding of problems that take place in public spaces in the daytime than, for example, a local shop owner, or the chair of a residents' group. Areas perceived as being high risk – 'risk perception hot spots' – are often correlated with crime hot spots, but not always. This disparity underlines that the issues that signal risk to residents may not be those that register as issues for the police. Engagement with the community through multiple methods can help identify these differences.

However, there are issues with innovative methods of engagement as well. All engagement work is resource-intensive but efforts such as door knocking are particularly so. There is very little specialist training for community engagement, even through the PEQF, meaning that it can be hard for officers to learn best practice (Lister et al, 2015). Some problems for more innovative engagement activities are similar to those for public meetings. Innovative community engagement can be 'limited in its ambition' (Lister et al, 2015, p2) and focused more on information gathering than preventive problem-solving, and can easily be disrupted by urgent work or abstraction (Higgins, 2018). This reiterates the need for officers to consider the purpose of engagement when making a plan, but also underlines the necessity of officers considering their own resources, and what can be achieved given the constraints within which teams operate.

Finally, as with the NRPP evaluation, it is sometimes difficult to disaggregate innovative engagement methods from the resources invested in publicising these methods. It was not always clear in the NRPP evaluation whether the teams that did best did so purely because they reached beyond public meetings; or because they had dedicated resources towards publicising these efforts. The next section looks at communication, both traditional and through social media.

Communication and social media

The effects of good community engagement, and good neighbourhood policing, can be multiplied many times by telling people about it. For this reason, communication should be considered as a central part of community engagement and given just as much time and thought as other forms of engagement. Communicating what neighbourhood teams are doing should be thought of as part of the neighbourhood policing function, rather than allowing it to be rolled into general police communications. Communicating effectively about police responses to problems raised is an essential part of the problem-solving process (Clarke and Eck, 2005). The involvement of the community in various parts of the problem-solving process is explored in the next chapter.

Feeling well-informed about police activity generally supports public confidence in the police. There are exceptions: sometimes feeling well-informed can negatively affect perceptions of fairness (Bradford et al, 2009b), perhaps due to greater public knowledge of negative press stories and scandals affecting the police. This has become a particular issue in recent years, with the spillover effects of negative stories in other countries such as the US having a direct influence on the legitimacy of policing in the UK (Goldsmith and McLaughlin, 2022). The anger felt at incidents such as the death of George Floyd leads to 'context collapse' in which it becomes difficult to disentangle global outrage from local experiences. It is a challenge for forces to recognise and respond to points of convergence – where the issues raised elsewhere also highlight real issues here and now – while preserving internal understandings of distinctiveness and supporting police morale. However, neighbourhood policing is one of the best ways of establishing that difference among members of the public.

The type of information that the police give out makes a difference. Low-level communication about the criminal justice system does seem to improve confidence (Salisbury, 2004). Hohl et al (2010) found that the widespread delivery of newsletters containing information about what the police were doing to find out about public concerns, reporting police actions on these issues, and their successes, substantially improved public assessments of police community engagement – and served to 'buffer' levels of confidence in the neighbourhoods concerned from negative media coverage of policing and crime. Residents are often particularly interested in information about the places where they live, such as neighbourhood policing, police performance and crime prevention advice, as well as details of how they could get involved (Quinton, 2011). There is little evidence that this, or the provision of crime maps, increases fear of crime (Quinton, 2011).

There are a range of different means of communication. Traditional media outlets such as local newspapers should not be overlooked by neighbourhood teams as a means of sharing information, though forces will generally insist this should be undertaken in consultation with the organisation's media departments. In the NRPP, four of the six sites recruited dedicated media officers. This facilitated wide press coverage of the activities undertaken as part of the programme (Tuffin et al, 2006). In one site, the force communications officer set aside 30 per cent of her time to publicising reassurance work and managed to set up a joint newsletter with the parish council. In another site, a local newspaper featured a week-long story with two-page spreads covering local police activity (Tuffin et al, 2006). Others managed to get local weekly radio slots, as well as using church magazines, residents' association newsletters, community newsletters and local press.

While the print circulation of local newspapers has fallen considerably since the NRPP, digital circulation is more robust, and trust in local newspapers is very high, at 58 per cent according to a poll conducted by Opinium for the Public Interest News Foundation in 2021 (Tobitt, 2021). Local media stories are therefore a very good way of multiplying the effects of neighbourhood policing activity.

As suggested earlier, though, other forms of print media can be used effectively to support neighbourhood work. Tailored local newsletters can increase confidence and perceptions of police–community engagement (Wünsch and Hohl, 2009; Hohl et al, 2010). However, there is also evidence that newsletters can have limited effects – especially when the target audience doesn't read them (Pate et al, 1986). Email newsletters can have very poor opening rates; and reach is often limited and not geographically well bounded. Handing pamphlets to residents on their doorsteps can increase their impact, but it is not clear if this is because the contact encourages greater readership (Singer and Cooper, 2009). One study suggested that very local newsletters, tailored for example to individual tower blocks, were well-received by residents, but this is very resource-intensive (O'Reilly, 2020). In London, Stanko and Dawson (2016) found that newsletters could improve public confidence, but (in an unpublished internal study) could damage trust and confidence if they did not appear to reflect residents' real concerns. Newsletters can therefore act as a multiplier of good face-to-face engagement, but cannot replace it.

Social media has increasingly been adopted both at force level and by local neighbourhood teams. However, consistent findings suggest that police forces tend to use social media in the same way as other media: to broadcast information rather than to engage interactively (Walsh and O'Connor, 2019). Research suggests that, while police officers often aim to break out of this 'broadcasting' pattern, for the most part, the practice of engagement has not been transformed (Bullock, 2018), in part because of organisational constraints and fears over the security and reputation of police forces being damaged by careless use of social media (Goldsmith, 2015).

A further limitation is often the social media channels used by police. Forces have often tended to focus their social media work on Twitter (Bullock, 2018), which has a limited audience and, despite common beliefs on the part of officers, is not particularly well-used by younger people (Bullock, 2014; Ofcom, 2018). While legitimacy can be increased by the use of Twitter, the effects are minor and it appears to be a result of increased transparency rather than participation, as interaction is very limited (Grimmelikhuijsen and Meijer, 2015). There is little specific guidance available to forces on how to use different channels, or the types of audience that can be reached through each; though this may be sensible given the pace of change in this landscape.

Some guidance on using social media is available for officers. The CoP has laid out six principles of engagement on social media in its Authorised Professional Practice (CoP, 2020). These state that officers undertaking online engagement need to be credible; consistent; responsive; an ambassador for the force; inclusive; ethical; and personable. These principles are intended to support procedural justice – by ensuring that officers are open, fair, honest and seen to be impartial – but also distributive justice, by making sure that digital engagement is understood as one tool among many, and that some residents (particularly the elderly) will not have access to the internet. It should also be borne in mind that even those who access the internet regularly may not seek out information about the police. Other, more traditional channels are still important to supporting public confidence.

Social media does, however, have real strengths as an additional strand. It can be used to support visibility, and accessibility, as noted in the last chapter – though for the best results, officers need to be able to access this using mobile devices while out in the community (Bullock, 2018). It can support the statutory requirement to supply residents with information about crime and disorder in their neighbourhoods, and to point residents to contact details not just for the police but for other agencies. It can help officers build up a 'community map' of a neighbourhood (CoP, 2018c). It may have particular strengths in reaching communities that are geographically dispersed, or who do not tend to attend meetings or read newsletters (CoP, 2018c); similarly, it can multiply the effects of other engagement such as email newsletters (O'Reilly, 2020). As discussed earlier in this chapter, it can be a good way of engaging communities when aligned with other methods, and can also support problem-solving through (for example) analysing what issues local people discuss in neighbourhood forums, or engaging with residents through those forums to help identify problems and solutions.

The best formula for good social media engagement will depend on the profile of the neighbourhood and a good understanding of how different groups engage with the police. Some forces prefer that the organisation's own communications specialists undertake the bulk of social media engagement (Ralph, 2022). However, this is better for information-sharing than engagement as such specialists will largely not have local knowledge. The 'humanising' effect of less authoritative communications (Ralph et al, 2022), and the use of humour (Wood and McGovern, 2021), can encourage residents to engage, and to have more positive interactions with the police. For neighbourhood police officers, therefore, a more relaxed and informal style, incorporating positive local stories, may be better to build the local relationships and engagement needed to support public confidence.

Summary

A substantial amount of legislation and guidance prevails upon forces to ensure that they engage with communities. However, the approach of more recent governments has been towards democratic accountability as a guiding principle. This means that, while there is now a legislative requirement to consult at neighbourhood level, the purpose of that engagement may be less clear. From a neighbourhood policing perspective, however, community engagement should always be seen in the context of supporting public confidence. As Chapter 3 discussed, this means trying to ensure that people feel their neighbourhoods, and their concerns, are being heard by police, and that officers are present and engaged.

The much maligned public meeting can be an effective means of public engagement; and even when poorly attended, its existence demonstrates to the public that the police are present in their communities and will be available when they are needed. Public meetings can help to support visibility and accessibility – especially in the absence of police stations, or restricted public hours – by providing a predictable and reliable channel for the public to find and talk to a police officer. They also require a relatively limited investment of resources compared to some other methods, and also allow a space for informal relationships to be built, through more relaxed conversations before and after the formal meeting. Ward panels or similar structures, which establish a core group of local residents who organise and chair the meetings, can alleviate pressure on officers. Such meetings can also play a role in community-building, discussed further in Chapter 8.

This in turn can free up neighbourhood officers to explore more innovative engagement methods. There is no single prescription for what works in a given neighbourhood, though 'outreach' seems an effective way of reaching hard-to-reach groups. The 'signals' of disorder felt by marginalised groups as symbolising disorder and undermining confidence may be different to those identified by those who are more vocal and articulate. However, this should not be at the expense of the issues raised by those who do engage with the police. There is a strong collective element to risk perceptions (Innes, 2005b), which means that there is often broad agreement between individuals about what the local problems are. Focusing on these signals is most likely to register with the wider public, and it is broader confidence that is the underlying purpose of neighbourhood policing.

Flexibility is key – methods of community engagement that succeed in one area may fail in another, and some groups may not see themselves as coherent communities at all (Myhill et al, 2003; Myhill, 2006). HMIC (2008) praised the way that many forces had asked local communities how they preferred to be engaged with, and recommended that engagement continue to be 'flexible and adapted to local circumstances' (HMIC, 2008, p25).

Finally the work done by officers needs to be publicised – an element of neighbourhood work that is often marginalised itself. Feeling well-informed about police activity is known to buffer public confidence, but it must reflect authentic community engagement, or it can have the opposite effect. Again, it is vital to think of neighbourhood policing in terms of its purpose, as a way of improving confidence through visibility, engagement and problem-solving. Keeping this in mind allows us to see communications as a way of facilitating that.

This chapter suggests that, in line with existing scholarship on confidence and legitimacy, good community engagement allows officers to demonstrate shared values. In broadcasting what they have done, they reflect high-quality engagement with the community to find out what was needed; in social media they behave with authenticity and respond to resident concerns. Community engagement is ultimately about building relationships with residents – and communicating that work is a central part of the task.

Questions for further consideration

1. If a forum isn't representative of the whole community, is it still a useful means of engagement? Why?
2. What is the value of accountability as a guiding principle of community engagement? What are its weaknesses?

Further reading
Bullock, K. 2014. *Citizens, community and crime control.* Basingstoke: Palgrave Macmillan.
College of Policing. 2018. *Neighbourhood policing guidelines: Supporting material for frontline officers, staff and volunteers.* Coventry: College of Policing.
Myhill, A. 2006. *Community engagement in policing: Lessons from the literature.* London: Home Office.

6

Solving problems

Introduction

Problem-solving was the third of the main 'mechanisms' identified through the early pilots of reassurance and then neighbourhood policing. As seen in Chapter 3, the results of the National Reassurance Policing Programme (NRPP) showed that problem-solving could make a big difference to communities, particularly if they were involved in the process, or if the problem was rooted in anti-social behaviour (Tuffin et al, 2006). Problem-solving was adopted as one of the three central processes of the new Neighbourhood Policing Programme in 2005.

'Problem-solving' as a model of policing has a longer history. Models of Problem-Oriented Policing (POP) were developed in the US in the 1970s and 1980s to encourage forces to move away from reactive responses to crime, and instead consider more proactive work. This was intended to encourage police to think of the 'unit' of police activities as problems, rather than crimes (Goldstein, 1979). This pre-dated the move towards community policing; and indeed, the early prescriptions for POP had little requirement for community input.

The new neighbourhoods thrust in the UK, by contrast, did insist that communities be involved. Problem-solving was intended to be an integrated process involving police and other agencies as well as local communities, at every step of the process. However, ensuring this happened in practice was more difficult. Not only did the early evaluations suggest that problem-solving activity might take longer to establish, and to 'cut through' with residents than other elements of neighbourhood policing (Quinton and Morris, 2008), there have been repeated accounts of difficulties with problem-solving, and many of these issues have been exacerbated by austerity. Problem-solving requires a long-term engagement with communities, strong relationships with partners, and the capacity and resources to focus on issues which may not appear high on strategic priorities: all this mitigates against problem-solving as a mechanism when budgets are tight.

However, more recently there has been a reinvigoration of problem-solving as an approach. This is in part due to the renaissance of the neighbourhood model, discussed in Chapter 2, and also as a result of a wider recognition that reactive models of policing fail to cope well with the range of demands on modern policing (Sidebottom et al, 2020). Problem-solving therefore remains at the heart of good neighbourhood policing, and this chapter explains why that is the case. It begins by discussing the roots of POP, and how it was intended to make the police more responsive to communities. It also touches briefly on critiques of the model – some of which suggest that POP is simply not ambitious enough.

The chapter then looks more deeply at problem-solving in neighbourhood policing specifically, and the importance of community involvement at every stage of this process. This speaks to the relationship between problem-solving and the signal crime perspective – but also why the involvement of the community in problem-solving needs careful management. This section concludes with an assessment of the way that the College of Policing (CoP)'s (2018) Neighbourhood Policing Guidelines treat problem-solving.

This segues neatly to a discussion of SARA as the dominant problem-solving model in British policing. SARA stands for Scanning, Analysis, Response and Assessment, and is the model recommended by the CoP and integrated into the Police Education Qualifications Framework (PEQF). This section gives a comprehensive account of SARA, breaking down each stage as a guide to practice.

Finally, the chapter looks at problems with problem-solving. These range from critiques of SARA as a model, and the feasibility of alternatives, to the long-established problems with implementation – particularly in the area of analysis. In particular the chapter considers the difficulties that can arise if problem-solving is regarded as 'police work' rather than a response to community signals, engaging the community at every stage, and the related need to manage expectations; the chapter concludes by reiterating that building trust as the basis of strong relationships has to be a key part of the problem-solving process and of neighbourhood policing work as a whole.

Problem-Oriented Policing

Problem-solving as a policing model is, like community policing itself, partly a response to the failures of 'professional' models, as discussed in the introduction to this book. In this context, 'professional' describes a model of policing introduced in the US which was deliberately intended to focus police work away from long-term immersion in communities, in order to limit corruption; and instead to focus police attention and activity on serious 'street crimes' such as bank robbery. This model encouraged a strict separation of policing activity: officers were no longer to live in the communities they policed, and were to prioritise policing in cars over foot patrol. Specialist teams were set up to make the investigation of serious crimes more efficient.

This 'professional' model led to the dominance of what Sherman (2013) describes as the three Rs – random patrol, rapid response and reactive investigation. The 'professional' model influenced policing strategy in the

UK as well; the 1960s and 1970s saw the increased use of Unit Beat Patrol in cars instead of foot patrol. As seen in Chapter 3, this contributed to the increased separation of police officers from the communities they policed, and also made it hard for forces to have a holistic sense of the intelligence and information being gathered by officers working in different parts of the force.

By the mid-1990s, partly prompted by some of the crises discussed in Chapter 3, and responses such as the Scarman report, British forces were beginning to change their approach. Firstly, in order to address the development of 'silos' within forces – where information was gathered but not shared between teams – some forces had begun looking at 'intelligence-led' policing models to better deal with serious and organised crime. The idea behind this was that information would be coordinated and better shared by structuring the way that information was gathered and processed (O'Reilly, 2021). In 2000, the National Criminal Intelligence Service implemented the National Intelligence Model (NCIS, 2000). This framework was specifically developed to try to break down those silos and ensure that information was available across team boundaries by restructuring the way that information was gathered and processed.

POP was aimed at making police less reactive (Goldstein, 1979). 'Problems' for Goldstein are recurring incidents that are of concern to the community, and which constitute police business; he argued that police should focus more on problems, rather than incidents (Goldstein, 1990; Cordner and Biebel, 2005).

Under the POP model, police first identify 'specific problems that the public expected them to handle' (Goldstein, 2018). This in itself was a departure from the police alone determining what they considered police business. There are a range of ways that the police could do this; such as analysing calls for service, or information drawn from other police data or agencies.

Police then systematically gather information about the identified issues, and target responses towards the aspects of the problem likely to benefit most from a policing response; thinking creatively about each possible way of responding. Forces were also encouraged to prioritise responses that focused on preventative action, moving beyond law enforcement and the criminal justice system. All responses needed to be rigorously evaluated (Goldstein, 1990; Bullock, 2010).

Goldstein himself was keen to see POP responses engage the local community and a range of other stakeholders (Goldstein, 2018). However, as a model, POP's focus is firmly on the behaviour of the police – other agencies are peripheral rather than central, perhaps understandably given the stringent separation of police from the public under the professional model in the US.

The POP framework put forward by Goldstein heavily informed the later development of neighbourhood policing (Read and Tilley, 2000; Bullock and Tilley, 2009). Problem-oriented policing and problem-solving are often used interchangeably. However, there are a number of critiques, which stem from two main sources: that Goldstein's idea of a problem was too narrowly defined; and secondly that the community engagement element of POP was too peripheral – a question turned to in the next section. Even advocates of POP acknowledge that it has not been fully integrated into policing and a range of explanations have been offered for this, from the particular culture of police organisations (Tilley and Scott, 2012), to the dominance of performance metrics which fail to fully measure the success of problem-focused approaches (explored further later in the chapter).

Some argue that expanding our understanding of what a problem is could help align problem-solving with the 'business' needs of policing (Borrion et al, 2020). Goldstein's understanding of a problem was itself an expansion of the role of the police, from responding to crimes to intervening in the causes of them. However, Borrion et al argue that this is insufficient, and the police need to encompass a wider range of consequences of an intervention, both positive and negative. This has merit for neighbourhood policing in terms of confidence and legitimacy. As this chapter argues, interventions need to be evaluated in the context of their wider purpose, not simply in terms of whether crime is reduced.

However, while an architect or an ecologist needs to consider the effects of their actions on unknown members of the public decades from the moment of decision-making, the police mission is both more constrained and less resourced. While the impacts of problem-solving measures might resonate in time and space beyond those who experience the immediate consequences of them, the purpose of neighbourhood policing is to focus on the effects of police action within their local areas and on local communities. The next section explores how neighbourhood policing departs from POP in one key element: the integration of the community into the problem-solving process.

Communities and problem-solving

POP as a model overlaps with many of the core aspects of neighbourhood policing. It focuses on problems rather than crimes; and it acknowledges that agencies other than the police might be better placed to deal with some of these. It also defines a problem primarily by whether communities believe there to be a problem. However, there are some important differences between the two models.

The first is focus. POP's focus is on problems themselves. The path to finding a solution to these might well involve engaging the community – especially at the early stage of identifying what the problem might be. However, neighbourhood policing's core focus is the relationships between the police and the public (Bullock, 2010); problem-solving is just one mechanism through which relationships and confidence can be built (Gill et al, 2014).

Secondly, POP relies on police judgement with regard to defining and resolving problems. It is the police who decide if problems defined by the community are in fact 'police business'. POP assumes that subjective experiences of crime and disorder are not a good guide to what police should prioritise, and that residents are likely to 'lack the kinds of information necessary to make informed decisions in regards to policing priorities' (Murphy and Muir, 1985, p70). Neighbourhood policing, by contrast, brings the community in from the beginning to identify problems; and, moreover, is explicit about the need to include the community in evaluating the results of problem-solving activity. In POP, this element is largely optional.

Collaborative problem-solving was emphasised from the beginning of neighbourhood policing: both in the government's 2004 White Paper *Building communities and beating crime* (Home Office, 2004a; Myhill, 2006) and in guidance made available to forces (ACPO, 2006). Neighbourhood policing teams were defined as taking 'an intelligence-led, proactive, problem-solving approach' (Home Office, 2004a, p7). Community involvement in identifying and resolving problems was explicitly set out as an essential element of successful neighbourhood policing in the White Paper: 'Your local officers will work with you and your neighbours to identify the most appropriate solution to the problem and work together with their partners in the local authority or other local agencies and communities themselves to deliver that solution' (Home Office, 2004a, p8).

This was cast as a return to the original principles of UK policing, in which the New Police were enjoined first of all to prevent crime, rather than simply to enforce the law after crime had taken place (Home Office, 2004a, p19). The White Paper also underlines that, while different models of approaching neighbourhood policing might be adopted, all effective models will involve local communities doing more than just identifying problems, but instead 'prioritising action and shaping and participating in solutions, along with police and partners'.

The signal crime perspective sees problems as issues that can be tackled with the help of members of the community with particular knowledge. Interestingly, as seen in the last chapter, this perspective means that it may not always be necessary to consult with a representative cross-section of the wider community, so long as 'key individuals' could be identified who had an in-depth knowledge of the relevant issues (Innes, 2005b; Bullock, 2010).

However, early neighbourhood policing guidance on involving the public warned of the risks of problems being defined by those who turn up for meetings, underlining a transition towards a more participatory conception of the consultative process, and a focus on problems, rather than signals (Forrest et al, 2005). This is an area where neighbourhood teams therefore need to take care, particularly where they have identified communities that are not always heard.

In principle, neighbourhood policing should involve the community at every stage of problem-solving, from identification of problems to resolving issues and evaluating interventions (Bullock, 2010). In practice, there are a limited number of ways in which citizens can legitimately participate in problem-solving (Myhill, 2006). This is reflected by the CoP's guidelines, which refer to two different approaches to problem-solving – community-led, and police and partner-led. The latter approach focuses on high-harm issues and vulnerability.

However, this does not mean that officers should revert to defining and tackling problems without community input. Such an approach risks prioritising police problems over community issues, and could lead to residents feeling that their concerns are being ignored. Problem-solving in neighbourhood policing, like visibility and community engagement, needs to be seen in the context of its core purpose: to support public confidence in policing; which means that, in many cases, effectiveness in reducing crime should be seen in as secondary to authentic engagement with the community. Neighbourhood teams therefore need to be careful to ensure that they focus on their core purpose, and must prioritise this over deferring to police or partner expertise.

Nevertheless, there are a number of possible reasons why the community may not want to be involved in solving local problems. People may be afraid to be seen talking to and working with the police (Singer, 2004). There may be a history of poor relationships between the police and local residents (Skogan et al, 1999). Promises may have been broken in the past by the police and by other public sector organisations; public involvement rests on building trust (Singer, 2004), which can be damaged by previous broken promises or failure to manage expectations (Skogan et al, 1999).

It may be particularly difficult to stimulate public involvement in policing in more deprived areas, as crime itself can lead to withdrawal from community life, and such neighbourhoods can themselves be minefields of inter-community hostility. There may not be a coherent 'community' for the police to mobilise to solve local problems. Nor will there necessarily be any inherent experience or capacity to take part in such activities – problem-solving therefore needs to be a developing process and expectations need to be carefully managed. The CoP's neighbourhood guidelines emphasise the systematic use of models such as SARA to structure the problem-solving process, and the chapter turns to this next.

SARA as a problem-solving model

SARA is now the dominant framework for problem-solving in British policing. This four-stage model – Scanning, Analysis, Response and Assessment – first developed in the Newport News police department by Eck and Spelman (1987), is now well established, despite attempts to improve upon it with a range of other models (Sidebottom and Tilley, 2011). SARA is recommended by the CoP in its Neighbourhood Guidelines (CoP, 2018c) and integrated as part of the PEQF curriculum taught to many new police recruits since 2020.

SARA is a model for the systematic identification, assessment and analysis of problems, and the response and evaluation of those problems. It has four stages:

1. Scanning – identifying and prioritising the potential problem.
2. Analysis – thoroughly analysing the problem using a variety of data sources.
3. Response – developing and implementing interventions designed to solve the problem.
4. Assessment – assessing whether the response works.

Scanning

The process of 'scanning', stage one of the SARA model, initiates the SARA cycle illustrated earlier (Eck and Spelman, 1987). This process involves identifying recurring problems; prioritising the problems that have been identified; confirming that those problems really exist; digging more deeply to find out how often the problem occurs, and how long it has been a concern; and selecting problems for closer examination (Eck and Spelman, 1987; ASU Center for Problem-Oriented Policing, nd).

The SARA model draws heavily on Goldstein's definition of a problem; that is, a cluster of similar, related or recurring incidents rather than a single incident; a substantive community concern; and a unit of police business. It is up to the police to determine what a problem is, however, and whether a problem is real, an issue touched on in the last section and which the chapter will return to later on.

There are a number of common ways of involving the public in scanning for problems, and their analysis, including surveys, public meetings, focus groups and citizens' juries or panels (Forrest et al, 2005). Innovative tools that could be added include environmental visual audits, door knocking, diaries and micro-beats (Forrest et al, 2005). However, officers need to be clear and transparent with regard to the purposes of engagement. They also need to be authentic: involving the public in a superficial or tokenistic way can limit or even neutralise the benefits.

Analysis

The second stage of the cycle is the 'analysis' stage. This involves the identification of the events that preceded the problem, and the conditions around it; working out which data might need to be collected; researching what's already known about this particular type of problem; looking at how police usually address this problem and what the limitations are of that response; narrowing the scope of the problem as much as possible so that a specific issue can be addressed; finding as many resources as possible that can help; and trying to come up with a 'working hypothesis' – a best guess, that can be later proven or disproven – about why the problem is happening in the first place (Eck and Spelman, 1987; ASU Center for Problem-Oriented Policing, nd).

Analysis is an important part of the SARA process that can sometimes be overlooked as officers move straight to response. However, the evaluation of the NRPP found that the most successful problem-solving with regard to 'juvenile nuisance' often had detailed analyses of location, victim and offender (Tuffin et al, 2006).

There are a range of resources that officers can draw on during the 'analysis' stage. This could include turning to the force's own analysts; but could also involve research on the part of officers themselves. There are a number of databases of information to which officers have access, from the CoP's Crime Reduction Toolkit (CoP, 2022) to the Center for Problem-Oriented Policing based at Arizona State University (ASU Center for Problem-Oriented Policing, nd) and the matrix of evidence-based policing maintained by the Center for Evidence-Based Crime Policy at George Mason University, also in the US.

The CoP describes access to skilled analysts an 'essential' part of neighbourhood policing (CoP, 2018c, p31), describing its absence as a major barrier to problem-solving. However, it also recommends that officers, staff and volunteers should have access to analytical tools and be able to think analytically in order to take ownership of this stage of the process themselves. The types of analysis recommended include statistical analysis, hot spot mapping, network analysis and examining social media and big data. Thinking analytically includes challenging assumptions, including about the causes of problems and who the perpetrators might be; developing and testing theories; exploring the evidence base; and taking the initiative to interrogate force and partner data (CoP, 2018c, p33).

Officers should also consider taking an inventory of how similar problems are being addressed by their own force. An inventory of this sort should go beyond a simple list to think about the strengths and weaknesses of such approaches. The approaches currently being taken may have limitations – if they worked perfectly, the problem identified wouldn't be a persistent problem – so officers should attempt to identify what doesn't work and why.

Response

In the SARA model it is only at the third stage that officers respond to problems. This is more than simply choosing a method of responding and implementing it. Responses to an identified problem need to be planned systematically. The stages of 'response' include brainstorming for new interventions; considering what other communities with similar problems have done; and only then choosing among the alternative interventions on offer, drawing from the ideas thrown up during the analysis stage as well. Officers then need to outline a response plan, and to identify who is going to be responsible for each stage of the response. Only then, in the final stage, do officers and others actually carry out the planned response to the problem.

Brainstorming is often considered as a very creative way of gathering ideas. However, group brainstorming suffers from a number of issues (Furnham, 2000). These include social loafing – individuals make less effort when in groups; evaluation apprehension – a fear of suggesting ideas in case you feel stupid; and production blocking – not speaking because someone else jumps in. Research has suggested that individuals working alone can come up with twice as many ideas as those in groups, and they are rated as more feasible (Furnham, 2000). Instead of group brainstorming, then, a better way of gathering ideas is to start with individual brainstorming; then using wider groups to build acceptance for those ideas, and using 'mediated criticism' to develop them. These brainstormed ideas should also be compared with, or include, the ideas drawn from the research undertaken during the analysis stage.

As noted earlier, the response plan needs some consideration. Any response requires specific objectives, or there will be no way of evaluating whether it has worked. Officers should also identify who is going to be responsible for implementing each part of the plan – particularly if it involves non-police partners. If this is not ascertained and agreed early on, there can be a number of consequences: this can include confusion as to whose job it is to implement an element of response; a lack of accountability; a loss of trust between partners; a failure to fully respond to the problem, or to respond at all; and quite possibly the responsibility for the entire response falling on the shoulders of officers (O'Reilly, 2020). Only when all of these elements have been undertaken should officers begin to implement their plan.

Community involvement in response is largely limited to surveillance and crime prevention, but Forrest et al (2005) also list interventions such as 'local action teams' formed to deal with specific problems; community 'speedwatch' schemes; and resident involvement in activities such as community clean-up days.

Assessment

The final stage of SARA is assessment. This stage is where officers should evaluate the problem they have tackled and the response that they have implemented, to ensure that it met the objectives set, worked as planned and didn't introduce new issues. It has two stages: process evaluation and impact evaluation. The first is to determine whether the plan that was laid out was actually implemented – without this, we cannot know whether the results were related to the plan or simply coincidental. This is known as a process evaluation. The second stage is to look at qualitative and quantitative data from before the response was implemented and afterwards. This is to determine whether the broad goals of the plan were met, but also whether the specific objectives laid out under the response stage were met as well. Then officers need to return to the original plan to see if there are any new strategies that are needed (Eck and Spelman, 1987; ASU Center for Problem-Oriented Policing, nd). Assessment is therefore an ongoing, iterative process – one that is more like a cycle than a straight line.

In a process evaluation, the key question is: 'Was the intervention implemented as planned and how was it altered for implementation?' This requires officers to look at what has been done and, regardless of results, to ask what went well and what didn't go well and the reasons why. A process evaluation focuses on the resources that were employed by the response (inputs) and the activities accomplished with these resources (results), but it doesn't examine whether the response was effective at reducing the problem (outcomes) (Clarke and Eck, 2005) – that comes next. When undertaking a process evaluation, officers should think about what obstacles arose, and in what way the response diverged from what had been planned.

The impact evaluation is the stage in which the results are examined. Impact evaluation addresses two main questions:

- Has the problem declined following the response?
- Did the response cause the decline, or was it something else?

The second question is more complex than the first as there can be more than one explanation for a change in a problem – for example, if officers have been undertaking extra patrols to try to reduce thefts of garden furniture, and the number of thefts has dropped off, is that because of the patrols? Or is it because it's now October and people have put their garden furniture away? Sometimes individual offenders can cause a disproportionate number of problems in a neighbourhood – the removal of a particular offender may have caused the problem to be resolved. Without this analysis, it is possible for officers to draw conclusions about their actions that aren't correct.

Finally, assessment processes must be ongoing. Officers need to review the original plan but also review the problem and its context. There might be some unintended, or sometimes expected, consequences and side effects of the response. Displacement and diffusion are two common consequences after implementing a solution to a specific problem; officers should also keep in mind that offenders can switch targets, change their tactics or change crimes.

Problems with problem-solving

Although SARA is dominant in British policing, it is not always clear to what extent it is fully incorporated into policing practice. Tilley (2010, p186), for example, has warned that its use is often 'rather desultory and formulaic'. Tilley notes that other disciplines such as engineering place more emphasis on the recursive or iterative nature of the problem-solving process – something that is often lost with SARA, which tends to be interpreted as a simple stage-by-stage model with a clear start and finish.

SARA is also not a perfect fit for neighbourhood policing. Though Tilley critiques SARA for its flaws in operationalising the problem-oriented approach, the SARA process is nevertheless drawn from POP and, as such, diverges in important ways from the principles of neighbourhood policing in terms of the integration of the community at each stage. While officers are encouraged to refer to the community, the model itself relies on police officers to determine the extent to which (for example) a problem is 'real'. This is an issue in the same way and for the same reasons as Innes (2005b) critiqued the POP model for prioritising problems over signals that were discussed earlier: it can lead to police ranking problems by the seriousness accorded to them under legislation, rather than the extent to which they make people feel unsafe or cause them to have less confidence in the police.

OSARA and other models

Some have attempted to revise or move beyond SARA. As of 2019, at least seven forces have adopted an extended SARA model known as OSARA. This model includes an extra stage at the beginning, where O stands for Objective. The principle is that the objective of problem-solving activity should be established before beginning to scan. However, there appear to be a range of understandings of the objective stage. Sidebottom et al (2020) found that some forces insisted that objectives be set in advance of scanning, while others that they be outlined on completion of the analysis stage. It is unclear how objectives could be sensibly set before scanning and analysis of a problem takes place.

Some forces have also begun to use alternative models such as PANDA (problem, analyse, nominate, deploy, assess) (Ratcliffe, 2018) and the National

Decision Model as frameworks for problem-solving (Sidebottom et al, 2020). In the early days of problem-solving, Read and Tilley (2000) suggested a model called PROCTOR, which set out the stages of PROblem, Cause, Tactic/Treatment, Output and Result. More recently, a model called SPATIAL has been suggested which builds on the SARA model, breaking three of the stages into two: Scan becomes Scan and Prioritise; Respond becomes Task and Intervene; and Assess becomes Assess and Learn (Burton and McGregor, 2018). However, there has been little take-up of these alternatives to date; and with the SARA model now enshrined in the UK's PEQF curriculum it seems likely that other models will find it difficult to make headway.

Implementation

There are consistent identified weaknesses in implementation of problem-solving (Bullock et al, 2021). Officers can be less than systematic in their initial analysis of problems. Officers sometimes make assumptions about the cause of a problem, or fail to check that a problem really exists to be resolved. For example, forces can assume a nationally identified problem exists locally (Read and Tilley, 2000). Her Majesty's Inspectorate of Constabulary (HMIC) noted in a thematic report, *Anti-social behaviour: Stop the rot*, that anti-social behaviour was often regarded as a 'second-order' problem which could easily be overlooked by officers who preferred to focus on criminal offences (HMIC, 2010).

Analysis is also often flagged as a weakness. The analysis of problems needs to be systematic and draw on a range of information. However, it is common for analysis of 'problems' to be limited and largely focused on police data and statistics, and for problems to be defined too broadly (Cordner and Biebel, 2005; Bullock and Tilley, 2009). Other weaknesses included use of only the most short-term data, when long-term analysis is likely to bring more benefits (Clarke and Goldstein, 2002), and failure to properly examine the source of a problem (Read and Tilley, 2000). As noted earlier, studies find that officers tended to 'jump to the response' (Sidebottom and Tilley, 2011, p16) before a proper analysis has been completed.

Officers can also be tempted to rely on personal experience when considering responses to problems, and are more likely to informally discuss problems with other officers than to search out research evidence on what might work (Read and Tilley, 2000). This can lead to an over-reliance on interventions based on traditional responsive policing, such as high visibility patrols and arrests. There can also be failures to fully plan out how measures could work in practice or to think about why responses would work. The implementation of problem-solving models requires that officers in neighbourhood roles take on considerable discretion to tailor solutions to the particular area's needs. Some officers can find this threatening – senior officers need to sacrifice control, while junior officers need to take on elements of strategic responsibility (Leigh et al, 1996). Managing expectations can also be tricky – there can be a sizeable 'expectations gap' between public demand and the level of policing that forces are in general able to provide. Limited resources must be linked to limited aims, or the resource will be stretched too thinly; and the limitations of projects must be made clear to all stakeholders from the beginning (Crawford et al, 2003).

Finally, the monitoring and evaluation of problem-solving interventions is rarely undertaken effectively (Bullock and Tilley, 2009). Systematic evaluation has generally been found to be weak, often using selective evidence and failing to consider alternative explanations or why an intervention might have had a given effect (Read and Tilley, 2000).

Many of the problems in embedding problem-solving can be traced to organisational factors, some of which are beyond the scope of this book. These include management commitment to problem-solving as a philosophy of work, and the hierarchical nature of policing, as well as the difficulty of producing measurable outcomes (Bullock and Tilley, 2009). The reactive nature of policing can also lead to short-term 'containment' of issues rather than long-term resolutions (Sidebottom and Tilley, 2011). Other issues include an absence of analytical capacity, and data sharing, issues that retain their relevance in the context of enhanced privacy rules such as the General Data Protection Regulation and budget cuts to support staff. The abstraction of officers from neighbourhoods was identified as an issue for the success of problem-solving by HMIC in 2008. Finally, a lack of dedicated, protected time to undertake problem-solving was cited by officers, especially those who also had response responsibilities (Read and Tilley, 2000; Colover and Quinton, 2018). This was particularly the case where problems involved engaging with the public or with partners.

Even what some term 'shallow' problem-solving (Braga and Weisburd, 2006) can have real benefits for everyday policing. To harness the full benefit of problem-solving as a mechanism for supporting confidence, it has to be incorporated into a wider philosophy of neighbourhood policing that prioritises working with the community. Building relationships between police and the community requires those relationships to be curated, and encourages the involvement of the public at every stage of problem-solving. However, a receding political emphasis on confidence in favour of harm-focused approaches may create an environment in which police expertise has the advantage.

Summary

The Neighbourhood Policing Guidelines published by the CoP specifically address recognised weaknesses of problem-solving at neighbourhood level, suggesting that structured models such as SARA be incorporated into problem-solving approaches (CoP, 2018a). However, and as the guidelines note, there are known implementation issues with problem-solving that require dedicated organisational and financial resources to solve. Problem-solving does not always produce measurable outcomes; it needs dedicated back-room analytical resources; officers need to be properly trained; and officers need to be given the time and space to do the work. Many of these issues are not just beyond the scope of neighbourhood teams but are beyond the control of the police.

Problem-solving often relies on the availability and engagement of partners (of which more in the next chapter). In brief, these need to have the capacity to step up to engage with the non-crime problems that police identify – in particular, local councils. Most police partners have suffered from significant budget cuts also, limiting their capacity to participate, let alone fill gaps left by the partial withdrawal of the police under similar constraints. Problem-solving is therefore peculiarly exposed to budget cuts, as it relies so much on collaborative working.

There are also grey areas in best practice. It is still not clear why problem-oriented policing works in some times and places, and not others (Tilley, 2010); moreover, there are no hard and fast rules for the balance that needs to be struck between identifying problems through sound data analysis and responding to problems identified by the community.

However, by approaching problem-solving through the prism of neighbourhood policing, there are some conclusions to be drawn. These conclusions are possible because (and unlike policing more generally) neighbourhood policing has a clear purpose: that of supporting public confidence. Confidence in the police is trust that the police (and the state as a whole) will defend local order, norms and social connection; so, too, problem-solving as a mechanism is at least as much about making the community feel that the police are concerned with keeping them safe as it is about actually fixing problems (though officers should fix them if they can).

This means that community interaction is important at every level of the problem-solving process. For example, assessing the effectiveness of a police response to a problem is important, but doing so without understanding whether the community believes it to have been effective presents a risk that officers may believe a problem is resolved when local residents do not. Similarly, managing expectations is crucial and something that cannot be done without the full engagement of the community at every stage. Negotiating expectations that can actually be met plays a central role in building trust between the police and the public (just as breaking promises can profoundly damage the legitimacy of local officers and 'the police' as a whole). This cannot be done at a distance or through data: officers need to be embedded with the community and need access to forums through which to have these conversations.

Problem-solving then should be seen as a mechanism that operates in concert with other mechanisms, and other people, rather than a policing model that can stand alone. This brings us neatly to the next chapter, which discusses the centrality of partnerships to neighbourhood policing.

Questions for further consideration

1. Should a problem only be defined as something that affects a community or should individual issues count? Why?
2. What does 'effective' problem-solving mean?

Further reading

College of Policing. 2018. *Neighbourhood policing guidelines: Supporting material for frontline officers, staff and volunteers.* Coventry: College of Policing.

Eck, J.E. and Spelman, W. 1987. *Problem-solving: Problem-oriented policing in Newport News.* Washington, DC: U.S. Department of Justice, National Institute of Justice.

Ratcliffe, J.H. 2018. *Reducing crime: A companion for police leaders.* London: Routledge.

Sidebottom, A., Bullock, K., Armitage, R., Ashby, M., Clemmow, C., Kirby, S., Laycock, G. and Tilley, N. 2020. *Problem-oriented policing in England and Wales 2019.* Coventry: College of Policing.

7

Partnerships

Introduction

Partnerships are central to neighbourhood policing. As seen in the last chapter, problem-solving in particular cannot be effectively undertaken alone. It is reliant on the police working closely with partner agencies whose responsibility it is to respond to many of the issues that are raised with the police. Residents do not always distinguish between the specific responsibilities of the police as opposed to local councils, for example. In raising issues, they are stating the existence of a problem that is affecting their sense of safety in their community. Good neighbourhood policing should therefore respond to these issues on these terms, while ensuring that these problems are passed to the partners who can resolve them.

Involving partners in crime prevention work has been encouraged in British policing since the 1984 issue of Home Office Circular 8/84 (Singer, 2004; Bullock and Tilley, 2009), which stated that many of the factors involved in crime were outside the control of the police, and thus 'all those agencies whose policies and practices can influence the extent of crime should make their contribution' (Home Office, 1984, cited in Singer, 2004). However, the last couple of decades has seen enormous growth in partnership working, to the point where it is now institutionalised.

This chapter begins with an account of that institutionalisation in policy, legislation and guidance, and the requirements placed on forces now to work in concert with other agencies. It unravels the narrative of partnership working from the early 1980s onwards, and describes the broad benefits that it was believed partnership work could provide for the police and other agencies.

Partnerships have now been embedded for sufficient time to have a good idea from research evidence about what makes them work effectively. The next section therefore looks at partnerships in practice, and the centrality of trust and continuity to ensure good relationships. Much evidence points to the importance of informal connections; and the chapter touches on the strengths and weaknesses of co-location as one means of embedding this. The chapter also looks at the problems inherent in partnership work, from the inconsistency in relationships that can stem from abstraction, to the difficulty of managing multiple expectations. Differences in working practices can often be at the root of failed partnership initiatives; but so too can governance and accountability structures, which are beyond the remit of the officers involved in the partnerships themselves.

However, one of the most pressing issues that recurs in partnership work – whether with other agencies or with the community – is value conflicts. These can arise between police and partners in the public sector, or between the police and community groups, but can also be encountered within communities, where different groups hold irreconcilable values (or, indeed, within the police). Confidence and legitimacy in part rest on the capacity to demonstrate moral alignment and to listen and respond to community priorities. Part of the remit of the neighbourhood officer, therefore, is to try to reconcile values that are fundamentally different. This chapter concludes by outlining a range of strategies often used by officers, and warns that the default tendency of officers to assume that police values and knowledge should take priority is a dangerous one for public confidence.

Partnership as policy

By the late 1980s and early 1990s it began to be recognised that the police could not reasonably be held solely responsible for crime levels; and that tackling crime and disorder needed to be the responsibility of more than one agency, working in concert. The Morgan report of 1991 identified a key lesson, dismissed by the Conservative government at the time (Crawford and Evans, 2017), but which has since become orthodoxy: tackling crime and its causes could no longer be the responsibility solely of the police. The Morgan report suggested a joint statutory duty upon the police and local authorities to work in partnership, which was later enshrined in policy by the New Labour government which came to power in 1997. New Labour's approach was explicitly focused on partnership as a way of governing. This encompassed joint working between the public and private sector; partnerships with communities; and, perhaps most importantly, partnerships between public bodies.

Initiatives to promote better working across the public sector had long been a feature of public policy in some areas such as health (Newman, 2001b). However, 'partnership' was distinctive in its response to the neoliberal changes introduced by the Thatcher and Major governments. It acknowledged the fracturing of policy delivery and the multiplicity of actors, particularly in the arena of community safety. It was also a recognition that many of the drivers of crime lay in areas well beyond police capacity to address alone.

This reflected a broader shift towards a focus on outcomes: 'What Works?' became a core driver of public policy. As discussed in Chapter 2, this pragmatic approach was married to a belief that a return to state-centred approaches was not politically feasible, but that the market-driven approach had also failed to deliver what it had promised. New Labour's approach was broadly aimed at steering rather than centrally directing public policy, and one of the means to achieving this was the breaking down of barriers to cross-sector working, and the establishment of structures to achieve this at a local level (Newman, 2001b).

Complex policy issues – such as crime and community safety – were seen as particularly appropriate for a 'joined-up' approach (Jessop, 2000; Newman, 2001b). This partnership working involved both vertical integration from the top to the bottom of the policy pyramid, and horizontal integration of the public sector with private and voluntary organisations, as well as communities themselves.

Partnership work in neighbourhood policing was recognised by Her Majesty's Inspectorate of Constabulary (HMIC, 2008, p35) as 'absolutely key to delivering success'. Partnership work with other agencies was not just desirable, but in many ways inevitable, not least because communities would often prioritise non-crime issues that could not be resolved by the police alone (Quinton and Morris, 2008, pp30–31).

In the UK, partnership working has been mandatory since the Crime and Disorder Act 1998. The Act, amended by the Police Reform Act 2002, made it a statutory requirement for 'responsible authorities' such as the police and local authorities to work in partnership with others, including the probation service and clinical commissioning groups, to reduce crime and disorder, by setting up Community Safety Partnerships. This was a formal acknowledgement that many of the causes and the consequences of crime fell outside the realm of the police (Crawford, 2001). This was supplemented by the £400 million Crime Reduction Programme (Bullock and Tilley, 2009), which was almost all aimed at partnership initiatives.

Local police constables were to become coordinators of an extended policing family (Crawford et al, 2005) which would include Police Community Support Officers (PCSOs), neighbourhood wardens, volunteers, security guards, and others, to create a 'mixed economy' of those delivering community safety services and residential patrols (Crawford and Lister, 2004).

Partnerships were to include the community as well. The 2004 White Paper laid out the government's belief in the ability of policing – and in particular, co-production within policing – to build community capacity (Home Office, 2004a). Similarly, the 2004 Strategic Plan also elaborated on the government's commitment to 'active citizenship' as part of the core business of the Home Office (Home Office, 2004b). Residents were envisaged as participating in a range of ways, from the more formal – local priority-setting – to the informal, such as 'looking out for neighbours' (Home Office, 2004b, p38). All of this was to contribute to 'building a community that upholds basic standards of decency and is strong enough to prevent and deter offending' (Home Office, 2004b, p38). The idea of active citizenship thus provided context for neighbourhood policing that did not need to engage everyone in the neighbourhood to be doing its job. Partial consent was enough.

The Crime and Disorder Act was subject to a major review in 2006. The amendments to the legislation introduced through the Police and Justice Act 2006 made a number of important changes to how Community Safety Partnerships (CSPs) worked. Responsible authorities were expanded to include Fire and Rescue Authorities, while more flexibility was introduced in how CSPs worked. The government also added in new responsibilities, requiring CSPs to focus more on drug taking and dealing and anti-social behaviour – as well as to implement the police National Intelligence Model within the partnerships in order to facilitate information-sharing (Home Office, 2006). The review also identified the need to make sure that CSPs undertook consultation, reporting to the community, rather than annually to the Home Office.

These changes were intended to make sure that CSPs were more responsive to communities, and in some cases the requirement to consult helped lock in the relationship between CSPs and other local bodies. In London, for example, the local Community Safety Partnerships often work in tandem with Safer Neighbourhood Boards, set up by the Mayor of London. These often (though not always) include representatives from local ward panels, which are in turn bodies set up by the Metropolitan Police Service but run by local communities which help set local priorities. In this way, the needs of local communities can be filtered up to strategic decision-making levels.

There are many other statutory partnership arrangements that have relevance to neighbourhood policing. These include Local Safeguarding Children Boards, set up under the Children Act 2004; Safeguarding Adults Boards, set up under the Care Act 2014; and also Multi-Agency Public Protection arrangements, often referred to as MAPPA, which were set up under the Criminal Justice Act 2003, and which bring police, probation and prison services to work together to manage offenders. Local criminal justice boards (LCJBs) are currently non-statutory, though the 2022 review of PCCs suggested that they should be moved onto a statutory footing. LCJBs are intended to bring together local criminal justice agencies, such as police, the Crown Prosecution Service, courts, probation, prisons and Youth Offending services. These often undertake work such as directing Integrated Offender Management activities. All of this work establishes important relationships which can be used in effective neighbourhood work; for example, when a known offender is released from prison and returns home.

This range of agencies and statutory partnership bodies demonstrates the importance of partnership working at a strategic level, and also that this has been recognised by successive governments. However, as the last section demonstrated, the last Labour government also paid particular attention to the role of partnerships – usually non-statutory – in neighbourhood policing. Towards the end of New Labour's time in power, increasing emphasis was also placed on Neighbourhood Management; a way of tailoring key services to the needs and priorities of a particular area and community in part through the establishment of Neighbourhood Managers to oversee partnership working in a given area (Turley et al, 2012). While long-term funding for such projects become considerably thinner on the ground after the 2010 change of government, the impetus of practice is still towards closer relationships between public and third sector agencies on the ground.

Partnerships are crucial to many different areas of neighbourhood policing, as has been discussed in the last several chapters. Partners can support visibility and even accessibility through patrols on the part of the 'wider police family'; this can sometimes pre-empt problems where neighbourhood wardens, for example, working for local authorities, can resolve issues directly. Partner work can enhance community engagement through providing extra conduits for talking to communities or hosting and being present at police–community events, and sharing information between agencies and with the public. Partners can have important data and can take on much of the work that community engagement and problem-solving activities generate. Partnerships are particularly important with preventative work, but partners can be engaged across the spectrum of neighbourhood policing activity. The next section explores what helps to make this work.

Partnership in practice

Partnerships have been established as part of police practice now for long enough that there is a good evidence base on how to make them work. Much of this is general but still relevant to neighbourhood work. This section explores some of the key lessons around trust, continuity, working styles and co-location, before turning to the specific challenges raised by working in partnership with local communities.

Trust is regularly cited as the single most important factor in effective partnership work. It is possible to operate in partnership in low trust environments; however, evidence suggests that these relationships lack creativity, are less effective and are reliant on formal structures (Brewer, 2013). Building trust as part of partnership working is an iterative process that is based on relationships. It cannot be developed in the abstract, but only as a result of continued encounters.

It is very hard to build trust over a short period of time. One of the most consistent factors in evidence about successful partnership working is the importance of consistent relationships. Informal relationships underpin many of the most successful partnerships (McCarthy and O'Neill, 2014) – officers and partners need to know that they can pick up the phone to each other, or have a chat at the end of a formal meeting, to discuss knotty issues in an atmosphere of trust. Trust is not something that can be handed over to successors in a role; it must be built up between named individuals. Thus time in role is crucial to effective partnership working.

While this is often an organisational issue, and therefore beyond the capacity of officers to address, an understanding of its centrality can help make existing partnerships a success. For example, where possible within a team, the same officers should deal with the same partners, rather than attempting to establish shared responsibility. Even shared inboxes should be dealt with carefully so that important one-to-one relationships are not undermined.

Time in role is an important element of continuity in relationships, but it contributes to successful partnership working in other ways too. Working in a partnership environment can be very different to the way of working within a police culture. Partners will have different organisational values – for example, they may be more welfare-oriented, or their organisational cultures may be more discursive, or focused on democratic accountability, which can slow decision-making (Read and Tilley, 2000). Experience in partnership environments can help officers understand that – for example – a lack of a clear task orientation may be a result of a culture that values compromise. For these reasons, McCarthy and O'Neill recommend that officers new to partnership working should be 'socialised', for example, by being briefed by and shadowing more experienced officers.

Partnerships themselves need to develop a distinctive working style. This needs to be inclusive: if some decisions are made by smaller groups within the partnership, then what McCarthy and O'Neill (2014) describe as a 'communication loop' must be established to draw in other partners – especially if there are implications of decisions for the partners themselves or the people they deal with. The working style of a partnership may also have to be adaptable; police are often dominant in partnerships, but effective partnerships require that many voices are heard. However, there may be circumstances when the police need to lead the response for reasons of mandate (police have coercive powers which partners lack) or of legitimacy – where the public expect the police to lead, for example, in dealing with anti-social behaviour (Innes and Weston, 2010). Some forces have developed joint working – for example, as of the College of Policing (CoP)'s practice stocktake (2015b), Durham had integrated joint training and development with partners, and the writing of joint policies.

Co-location is an increasingly popular way to embed partnerships and has been adopted in many areas. In the CoP's practice stocktake, the majority of force respondents said they had co-located staff, largely with local authorities – though some forces had pursued more innovative partnership strategies. Several forces had seconded officers to work with local authorities; some had co-located or established close working relationships with organisations such as transport services or within the voluntary sector.

Co-location is often an effective way of working: evidence demonstrates that physical proximity can enable information sharing, informal relationship building and, hence, trust, and can build the capacity to pool resources and draw on a wider range of expertise. However, co-location is not a panacea, and can build tensions where relationships between officers in the hub and those outside (whether police officers or other partners) become strained (O'Malley and Grace, 2021) as the informal relationships between officers co-located in a hub and those remaining in their stations are disrupted. Caution must be taken that the co-location hub, developed to break down silos, does not become a silo in itself (O'Malley and Grace, 2021); or that lack of trust in one agency damages trust in others (Turley et al, 2012).

Finally, the particular demands of working in partnership with communities needs to be addressed. While much of the early rhetoric of New Labour spoke of community partnerships, in practice there was little specific guidance that talked of how to do this in terms of a partnership, as opposed to as a facet of community engagement or problem-solving. The last chapter discussed the importance in problem-solving of managing expectations. In a similar vein, officers need to be explicit when partnering with communities about what can be expected from such partnerships. Some elements of police work are well-suited to formal and informal partnerships with community groups, setting local priorities and gathering intelligence. Others, however, are less so, and effective partnerships need to establish from the beginning what element of 'steering' and 'rowing' is involved (Harkin, 2018).

One way of building support for partnerships, and therefore the commitment to them outlined earlier, is to stress the pragmatic benefits outlined earlier in the chapter – the benefits of pooling resources, the increase in efficiency, and the enhanced capacity that partnerships allow to deal with the causes and not just the consequences of crime and disorder. As McCarthy and O'Neill put it (2014, p246), officers need to celebrate their successes and the practical benefits of partnerships, rather than to dwell on the difficulties. This is not however to suggest that problems should be overlooked. This next section looks at some of the common problems that are likely to arise.

Problems in partnerships

Some of the issues with partnerships that were common in the early days of inter-agency co-operation have been mitigated by familiarity – police officers and their partners are simply much more used to working together than they were in the 1980s and early 1990s. For example, many of these projects were dependent on short-term funding with no long-term vision or wider remit. Interagency tensions based on mutual misunderstandings and expectations were also more common. However, since the instigation of the Neighbourhood Policing Programme, partnership working has become institutionalised, and has been one of the more resilient elements of the model even in a context of budget cuts for both police and partners (McCarthy and O'Neill, 2014). It has also been internalised by forces, and is now more likely to be broadly supported at both strategic and operational level (McCarthy and O'Neill, 2014).

However, that is not to say that issues no longer arise. Many of the problems that arise in partnership working come from an absence of the factors mentioned in the last section. There are a number of sources of such tensions. They can stem from poor or under-developed relationships between partners, leading to a lack of trust; from organisational issues such as abstraction that disrupt partnership working; from differences in governance and accountability between partners, and external to them, which can sometimes disrupt co-working; and from cultural issues that can lead to misunderstandings.

Trust is central to good partnership relationships. However, inconsistent relationships, ignorance about each other's roles or lack of experience can all damage trust or prevent it being developed. Problems can arise where officers are very new to the role or have not been sufficiently 'inducted' into understanding the way that their partners do business (McCarthy and O'Neill, 2014). A lack of staff continuity is consistently identified as a major barrier in partnership working, particularly at the neighbourhood level (Turley et al, 2012). This could be exacerbated if new members of staff were not as committed to or experienced in collaborative working. Neighbourhood teams need to think carefully about how they manage staff turnover, given the centrality of continuity to building trust between partners.

In partnerships, as in all problem-solving, expectations need to be managed. Objectives need to be specific, achievable and realistic. The police cannot realistically always respond, as Bittner put it, to 'something-that-ought-not-to-be-happening-and-about-which-someone-had-better-do-something-now!' (2005, p161). There is a limited amount of literature looking specifically at how the police and partners deal with residents' expectations. In Chicago, Skogan et al (1999) found that previous broken promises had damaged problem-solving capacity, while Singer (2004, p73) speaks of the years of 'perceived and real neglect' in the areas where his pilot reassurance programme was undertaken, and the related necessity to not over-promise to residents. The existence of the Neighbourhood Policing Programme in itself may have raised public expectations (McLaughlin, 2008); something also noted in New Earswick (Crawford et al, 2003). This is something of general concern in a context of straitened resources. However, announcing the limits of police capacity risks encouraging crime and endangering public confidence. Managing expectation and demand on the police is therefore a very risky business.

Organisational issues can exacerbate both the difficulties in establishing and maintaining continuity, and the capacity to manage expectations on the part of partners and the community. HMIC also found a large amount of abstraction among neighbourhood officers; between half and two-thirds of police constables were being abstracted once or more a week; one-fifth were being taken away three times a week or more, essentially no longer being able to perform their neighbourhood policing function. Even PCSOs were taken away from neighbourhood work, one-third at least once a week (HMIC, 2017).

Good neighbourhood work relies on extensive local knowledge, which requires continuity in post; but partnership working relies on this even more so. For example, ward panels in London could support many aspects of neighbourhood policing, but rested on long-term relationships built between panel members, partner agencies and police officers (O'Reilly, 2023). These are the kinds of relationships that can be easily damaged by abstraction of police to other duties or to high turnover, the latter of which is an increasing issue as budget cuts lead to council restructuring as well as reductions in police numbers. Community cohesion work in Luton was undermined by a 'lack of a consistent and familiar neighbourhood policing presence' (Higgins and Hales, 2017, p11), with the absence of continuity leading to the erosion of working relationships, and ultimately, resistance to partnership work itself (Higgins and Hales, 2017). Coordination between local neighbourhood teams and other specialist departments can also suffer for a lack of continuity in supervision (Higgins, 2018). There can be difficulties in formulating clear objectives for a team if there are multiple supervisors over a relatively short period of time.

Some tensions in partnership are derived from the structure of the partners involved in co-working, particularly with regard to accountability and governance; and are to some extent inevitable. For example, government ministers wanting quick results to show to the electorate may push for the rapid implementation of a promised policy, where the slow work of co-operation and co-production might have resulted in a better outcome. Partnerships can be pulled in different directions according to the particular model of governance under which they operate, and these different imperatives are not necessarily reconcilable. The police are tied to particular structures of accountability, roles and procedures, which can lead to tensions where more flexibility would be desirable; for example, working with communities who struggle to understand the limits of the police role. Accountability within partnerships – for example, ensuring that police are ultimately responsible for local priorities – can be seen by communities as limiting the pace of decision-making.

This is particularly the case for neighbourhood policing, because its partnerships are with the community and may also involve voluntary sector organisations, as well as having considerable links with local authorities. These groups are very different and have different needs and demands; as mentioned earlier, local authorities prioritise accountability and transparency in decision-making, but for voluntary and community groups, the formality that these demands engender may be exclusionary in themselves (Newman, 2001b). There can be particular tensions around the impetus on the part of both police and local authorities to control and regulate in contexts where communities expect co-production or the rhetoric of the partnership suggests empowerment – all of which demands a relinquishing of control, power and of expertise.

Finally, different cultural approaches can have a particular effect, and cultural differences can be particularly difficult to address. For example, the police are a famously pragmatic organisation; their primary impulse is to get things done. Partnerships between the police and local authorities can therefore struggle due to the overwhelming imperative within local government towards accountability. As one community safety director explained, 'The police want to do everything yesterday and the Local Authority have to go through three committees' (Hughes and Rowe, 2007, p332). The pragmatic imperative, particularly at a time of budget constraints and targets, may also limit the extent to which police are willing and able to take the time needed to embed networks and build consensus. A thrust towards pragmatism can also lead to a tendency towards marginalising difference and a directive style of leadership (Newman, 2001b).

This pragmatic bent also tends to encourage police officers to take charge in any situation. As noted in the last chapter, evidence on problem-solving initiatives suggests that the majority are police-centred. For example, Read and Tilley (2000) found that in just 5 per cent of initiatives reported by police forces were they the junior partners. Effective collaboration may require the construction of a new collective identity for the partnership (Hardy et al, 2005). However, it is not clear the extent to which the limits of the police 'form' permit the shedding of one identity and the construction of a different, more collective one (Harkin, 2015).

Partner organisations can often fail to understand each other's working practices (Read and Tilley, 2000; Hughes and Rowe, 2007). Crawford (1999) observes that much discussion on partnership working suggests that the partners in an enterprise are equal; but in fact, as the later New Earswick project demonstrated (Crawford et al, 2003), these differences can lead to judgements about each other's values. In New Earswick, for example, officers were resistant to attending the large number of time-consuming meetings held by the funders of the post, fearing (among other things) the likelihood of such meetings generating extra demand.

The practical outcome of this can sometimes be confused. The rhetoric of partnership working can underplay the plurality of some of the partners concerned: local businesses, for example, do not have identical interests (Crawford, 2001). This is equally true of the different tiers of local authorities, and the political interests within them; a Conservative-dominated County Council, with responsibility for neighbourhood issues such as highways and street lighting (and policing), may have different interests, priorities and available budgets than a Labour Party-dominated district authority whose members may have greater engagement with neighbourhood officers.

Many of these differences in organisational culture can rest on perceived – or indeed real, and deeply held – value conflicts, an issue turned to next. The multiple organisations and individuals involved often mean that partnership working can lead to the attempted incorporation of a wide range of goals and ideologies. This risks diluting the focus and effectiveness of initiatives, occasionally to the point where the purpose of the original initiative is lost. As Read and Tilley (2000, p31) warn, '[t]here is a risk that partnership in all things is fetishised as an end in itself'.

Managing value conflicts

The breaking down of silos between agencies has thrown up challenges for partnerships across the public sector. Many of these, as discussed earlier, relate to the challenge of reconciling competing values. This section reviews what is known about how public sector workers manage these conflicts and offers some guidance to neighbourhood police officers when they encounter them.

Value conflicts are often 'incommensurable' – that is, no matter how much discussion takes place, there is no permanent consensus possible that completely removes the conflict. For example, one common set of value conflicts that the police can encounter is with public sector and non-profit organisations whose focus is on the welfare of their clients. This can include social workers, probation officers and charities that work with offenders. An organisation tasked with supporting offenders may believe strongly that their interests, and the prospects for their rehabilitation, are best served by keeping them out of prison. The values of the organisation, likely shared by many of its workers, are to focus on these individuals and their needs. However, the values of the police may come into direct conflict with this, particularly if an individual is identified by other residents as being the source of anti-social behaviour, crime or disorder.

This has particular importance for neighbourhood officers, who spend much of their time developing relationships with partners, and can therefore encounter value conflicts more regularly than other officers. For example, as well as the type of tension that can develop between agencies mentioned earlier, neighbourhood police often need to work with community groups, whose priority is the interests of their very small area, rather than the wider mandate of the police. Similarly, private sector organisations will usually value the need to make a profit above other motivations (De Graaf et al, 2016).

Police officers are often given considerable discretion as to how they operate on the ground – they are 'street level bureaucrats' (Lipsky, 1980). The burden of 'coping' with this dissonance between values is often left to the individual. There are a number of different strategies that officers can use to try to reconcile these value conflicts in the short term (Thacher and Rein, 2004; Stewart, 2009), some of which are outlined here:

- Firewalls: this describes a way in which different parts of the same organisation take on different values, to minimise conflict within organisations and to allow other actors to deal with different sections of the organisation when values come into conflict.
- Bias: conflict is neutralised by simply refusing to recognise some values as important. By asserting the primacy of the organisation's values, conflict is avoided.
- Casuistry: this is where conflicts are navigated based on an individual's experience in similar cases.
- Cycling: some values are dominant for a short while, then they are sidelined and other values come to prominence.
- Hybridisation: this describes a way in which new values are incorporated into policies so none take prominence (but may still conflict).
- Incrementalism: gradually more emphasis is placed on one value rather than others.

It is useful for officers to be able to understand and identify choices that they may be making, and to consider alternative ways of dealing with value conflicts when they arise. One of the most common strategies used by police officers is 'bias' (de Graaf and Meijer, 2019). This is when officers, faced with conflicting values, decide to simply stick to those that they know and understand the best: the values of the police. The culture of policing is pragmatic, and there is an emphasis on getting things done. As noted in earlier chapters, police culture(s) often contains a strong bias towards action and a sense of mission (Loftus, 2009; Reiner, 2010). Policing is also very hierarchical, which means that junior officers may be hesitant to challenge organisational values supported by their superiors. Unsurprisingly, therefore, research suggests that, when faced with value conflicts, police will largely resolve them by defaulting to the values they already hold – for example, relying on police knowledge of crime to determine local priorities rather than those articulated by the local community (de Graaf and Meijer, 2019; O'Reilly, 2023).

Another common strategy among officers is hybridisation. Sometimes officers are faced with a conflict between two values that they rate very highly. In this case they may try to balance them through a hybrid policy; for example, by trying to pay equal attention to participation and representativeness in neighbourhood policing activities (de Graaf and Meijer, 2019; O'Reilly, 2023).

Studies of the implementation of evidence-based policing also call attention to the extent of casuistry in police behaviour. This means approaching conflicts on a case by case basis, based on personal experience. Many officers still see policing as a craft, in which personal experience on the street is more valuable than anything taught in a classroom (Constable and Smith, 2015). The last section noted that one problem in implementing problem-solving was the tendency of officers to rely on their own experience rather than to look for best practice or research.

Many of the value conflicts that officers will encounter have something in common. They are based on, or exacerbated by, the tension between the law enforcement purpose of policing, and the equally strong need to legitimate that coercive force. As Chapter 3 explored, confidence and legitimacy in the police is not just reliant on the effectiveness of police in enforcing the law – though that plays a part – but on the ability of the police to demonstrate that they are doing so in broad 'moral alignment' with the communities they serve. There is almost always a conflict in doing this: policing by consensus is never complete; there is always someone being policed (Reiner, 2010).

All of this is particularly important right now because of the tendency in recent years, imposed by reduced police budgets, to think about policing in terms of its 'core' purposes and activities. The risk in these circumstances is that police organisations lose touch with communities; and what remains is coercion with no legitimation. This can, perhaps, be seen in contemporary debates over the role of 'Stop and Search' in tackling the spike in knife crime (Deuchar et al, 2019), where the police value of reducing harm can come into conflict with community understandings of fairness.

The reconciliation of competing values is therefore of particular importance to neighbourhood police officers. Demonstrating 'moral alignment' means showing residents that the police care about the values that citizens hold, and that the police share those values. This does not mean that the police need to always fully resolve value conflicts. In fact, many of them, as mentioned earlier, will be of an enduring nature that cannot be fully resolved. Sometimes the police and local communities will believe different things are of a different level of importance; similarly, different groups within the same community may differ over fundamental values, and police officers need to find a way of reconciling those as well.

Officers should be aware of the range of these and that they are not 'commensurable' – there is not necessarily any means of permanently resolving these conflicts. They also need to be aware of the range of strategies that are available to them and that they may be using these already, unconsciously. In particular, the tendency of police officers and organisations towards 'bias' as a coping strategy is something to be conscious of. Instead, police need to work on engaging and understanding local values and being conscious of any conflicts, and the sometimes unconscious strategies used to manage them, when they arise.

Because police work rests on the capacity to use coercive force, it is particularly important that the need to secure legitimacy is prioritised. Police officers often have a strong sense of 'mission' (Reiner, 2010), which can often be expressed through strong ideas of right and wrong. However, neighbourhood policing is about supporting public confidence in policing and, for this, police need to be flexible and adaptable where possible to the values expressed by the local community.

Summary

Partnership working is now enshrined in police work, in legislation, guidance and practice. Partnerships are crucial to neighbourhood working and should be considered as having the same centrality as other mechanisms such as community engagement, visibility and problem-solving. Good partnership work can also enhance all of these, and reduce demand on neighbourhood teams by providing conduits for community engagement and problem-solving, multiplying police visibility and reducing demand on teams.

Good partnership work is difficult, however. Trust is central to all effective partnership work but it takes time to build up and is often reliant on informal relationships that can bypass formal structures. But for police officers, long-term neighbourhood working with no abstraction has increasingly become the exception rather than the rule. Without this continuity, however, partnerships can become strained, partners can lose touch, or misunderstand each other, or can be pulled in different directions by their own internal demands, governance structures, and organisational cultures and values.

This means that how to do partnerships effectively has to become part of the skill set that neighbourhood officers need to learn. Where possible, specific relationships need to be handed over when officers leave their neighbourhood roles. Handovers should include new officers spending extensive time shadowing existing officers, and getting to know the major partners and how they prefer to work. Partnerships must develop their own style of working, in which officers and partners learn to adapt to and respect the different organisational cultures and values that they encounter. Co-location is often effective in encouraging partners to shed their previous identities and build a new one; but officers need to make efforts to retain links – formal and informal – with officers in other locations.

There are times, however, when values cannot be reconciled. These conflicts must be managed. For police officers this can be particularly tricky, as the features of their own organisational cultures, structures and 'form' can limit the extent to which they are able to adapt or to challenge the internal values of their own organisations. Officers tend to default to regarding police values as inherently superior. But this can be a real issue in neighbourhood work. Partnership working more than anything else underscores the importance of relationships, of the affective nature of confidence and trust.

This in turn should prompt officers and police organisations to be careful of the innate tendency of police organisations to believe that there is only one set of values that should ever take primacy – those of the police. As seen throughout this book, reflecting community values is crucial to legitimacy and confidence. Confidence and legitimacy rest on officers being able to show that they share the values of local communities, and that they listen and respond to what the community cares about. This means that officers need to be aware of their own default responses to value conflicts, and prepared to sometimes prioritise community and partner needs. The next chapter looks at how this work can help strengthen those communities themselves.

Questions for further consideration

1. Should the police always take the lead in trying to resolve local problems? What are the benefits and problems in them doing so?
2. Are value conflicts between police and their partners inevitable? What are the implications of this for the way that police and partners work together?

Further reading

Crawford, A. 1999. *The local governance of crime: Appeals to community and partnerships*. Oxford: Clarendon Press.

Higgins, A. and Hales, G. 2017. *Police effectiveness in a changing world paper 4: A natural experiment in neighbourhood policing*. London: The Police Foundation. Available at https://www.police-foundation.org.uk/wp-content/uploads/2017/06/changing_world_paper_4.pdf [Accessed 28 August 2023].

McCarthy, D. and O'Neill, M. 2014. The police and partnership working: reflections on recent research. *Policing: A Journal of Policy and Practice*, 8(3): 243–253.

Newman, J. 2001b. Joined-up government: The politics of partnership. In L. Budd, J. Charlesworth and R. Paton (eds) *Making policy happen*. London: Routledge, pp194–200.

8

Building communities

Introduction

Good neighbourhood policing work can build public confidence in policing. However, it also has the potential to build stronger communities. This was recognised in the earliest days of reassurance policing, and in the various White Papers produced by the then-Labour government that set the context for the Neighbourhood Policing Programme. This chapter examines whether community-building remains a desirable or realistic goal for neighbourhood policing; the evidence around the contribution of community policing to social capital and collective efficacy; how police can contribute to stronger communities in the longer term, and whether this is simply too much of an extension to the police remit at a time of straitened resources.

The chapter begins by looking at the policy context for community policing. It outlines the role of community building in the early pilots of the National Reassurance Policing Programme (NRPP), where community-building was included as a specific outcome. It examines the policy and guidance on community-building of the early New Labour years and where it went; how austerity has affected government conceptions of the police role; and how the establishment of Police and Crime Commissioners (PCCs) has revitalised community-building, through their wider remit and the flourishing of public health approaches, as a desirable end to which policing can work.

It then explores the nature of social capital and the different types of capital that scholars have identified, and how neighbourhood policing fits into this. The chapter identifies ways in which neighbourhood policing can enhance 'bridging' and 'linking' capital, and the 'collective efficacy' of communities – but also the problems with measuring the strength of communities in this way. There is a possibility that in modern urban communities, a strong community is not one where residents physically intervene to prevent crime and disorder, but one where they are willing to call the police. This has implications for the amount of demand generated in the short term by improvements in local policing.

Longer-term demand also remains a concern for forces, however, and the next section outlines three emerging approaches to community-building. These are community resilience and resilience policing; public health approaches; and asset-based community development. What these approaches have in common is that police officers become facilitators of networks, rather than the central actors in interventions. Good neighbourhood policing work will already be including many of these activities; however, there is real potential within some of these for further development.

There is an argument that community development is beyond the remit of the police, who should focus only on crime and disorder. The final section examines these arguments, and the possibility that police are losing their capacity to undertake community work, through increasing reliance on data, and disconnection from communities and each other brought on by constant reorganisations. However, the book finishes on a note of optimism; concluding that despite the current crisis of legitimacy – and even perhaps because of it – forces are beginning to think about managing longer-term challenges, as well as the immediate demands of increasing public confidence. Both of these trends have the potential to support the enhancement and development of strong neighbourhood work and strong neighbourhoods.

Community-building in policy

Neighbourhood policing was a product of the belief of the New Labour administration in the power and importance of local communities. The Labour government believed that 'strong communities' were central to mitigating a range of social problems and that neighbourhoods, as the places where people lived, were the best places on which to focus to create lasting social change.

There have been critiques of this focus. Appeals to community are often part of a strategy of legitimation, the attraction of which rests in part on ambiguity (Fielding, 2005; Mackenzie and Henry, 2009). Community is an appealing idea perhaps because we always feel as though we have lost it (Glynn, 1986) – what Nisbet (1953) called 'the ideology of lament'.

It is also clear that 'community' is not always benign for everyone, and questions of power are often played down. A sense of community can develop in an antagonistic relationship to another 'community' within the same geographical location; thus Irving et al (1989) imagine Asian shopkeepers developing a high level of community because of a feeling of threat from groups of their neighbours. Some argue that the New Labour government simply underestimated the complexity of the local (Wallace, 2010). It is difficult to find it when you need it, to decide who are its legitimate representatives or to hold it stable (Hughes and Rowe, 2007).

However, 'neighbourhoods' remain the basic local unit of policing. There are practical benefits of geography as a guiding principle in thinking about community policing. Keeping command units coterminous with local government boundaries, for example, helps facilitate partnership work between police forces and local authorities.

It also reflects the way people experience policing: subjective security, a feeling of safety, is ultimately local and based on neighbourhoods, not crime figures. Despite considerable research and an increasing focus in the literature on 'affiliation-based' communities, facilitated by technology and not depending upon physical proximity, the recent pandemic underlined the importance of the local for the most fundamental needs of citizens: access to supplies, physical safety and a sense of identity. As such, the neighbourhood remains the site for most of our understanding of how communities work and the role of policing within this.

The original impetus for much of this was the early results of a number of pilot projects such as the NRPP, the story of which was told in Chapter 2. The objectives of the NRPP included 'improved social capacity' from the start, along with improvements in disorder, fear and confidence. The first evaluation of the NRPP showed some effects on social capacity and collective efficacy; however, these were limited. Improvements in trust were sustained into the second year, but no other programme effects, such as involvement in community or voluntary activity, were evident. The evaluation suggested that changes in social capacity might require a longer timescale and different activity with partners, but did not rule out such an outcome in the longer term (Tuffin et al, 2006).

Many areas of New Labour policy set out to address how the activities of the state – including the police – could contribute to building 'strong, active and empowered communities' (Home Office, 2004a, p39, para 2.24). Strong communities were seen as part of the solution to crime and social exclusion. The Labour government therefore underlined the importance of increasing the capacity of local residents to engage with the police, and the importance of citizens taking some ownership of the safety of their local communities, rather than leaving this all to the 'authorities'.

Responsibilisation is a critical theme in the development of community-building in Labour's policy. This is an extension of the idea that state action should start with the local, and should no longer involve the state simply doing things to people – what the Labour government, and its successors, have termed a 'passive dependency culture' (Home Office, 2004a, p39, para 2.24). Rather, citizens should increasingly take responsibility for their own lives and communities, supported by the state to the varying extent that this is needed. This was largely to be achieved through increasing the opportunities for the public to take part, through many of the mechanisms already outlined – determining local priorities, encouraging engagement, sharing best practice such as 'community guardians' (Home Office, 2004a, p40) – but also giving communities more powers.

Some of these themes have been picked up by subsequent administrations, such as the community trigger, floated in 2004 and implemented under the Anti-social Behaviour, Crime and Policing Act 2014. The 'trigger', otherwise known as the Anti-Social Behaviour (ASB) Case Review, provides for a review of an ASB issue if a certain threshold (of complaints, poor response and potential harm to victim(s)) has been met. Critics had argued that the thrust of New Labour's policies in general was misplaced, asking police to go beyond their remit and using the criminal justice system to attempt to achieve social policy outcomes better attempted through other means. Like neighbourhood policing itself, this conception of the capacity of the state to build communities was not abandoned by the incoming Conservative government, but the prescription to achieve it was rebadged to suit a different set of ideological beliefs: in this case, the need to roll back the state and make space for communities to step up.

The Big Society reforms of public services, and policing in particular, would involve the removal of ring-fenced resources in order to 'localise' power and choices about funding – for example, removing ring-fenced funding for Police Community Support Officers, and bringing in PCCs; attempting to limit the remit of the police and to recast them as 'crime-fighters' (May, 2011); improving the transparency of public services so ordinary citizens could act as 'armchair auditors' (Pickles, 2010).

However, the government appeared not to have considered the extent to which voluntary capacity – the Big Society it was hoping to grow – was often dependent upon non-statutory funding from local government, which suffered 40 per cent cuts in income on average. Far from encouraging a flourishing of the voluntary sector, charities were hit hard by this loss of funding and, with household incomes often also reduced, struggled to generate funds from donations too. Meanwhile forces had been forced to withdraw much of their neighbourhood presence, as discussed in Chapter 3.

Nevertheless, the establishment of PCCs meant that the flame of community-building as a function of policing has yet to be entirely extinguished – the remit of PCCs being (crucially) crime as well as policing. For example, PCCs are increasingly exploring public health approaches to the reduction of violence, a strategy which looks at the structural causes of violence such as social, economic and environmental factors. Despite profound changes to the funding and ideological underpinning of policing policy, there is still space for thinking of policing as something intricately tied to the success and failure of communities themselves.

Social capital and collective efficacy

The idea that crime and disorder might be a feature partly of the community rather than of individuals has its roots in early sociology. Social disorganisation theory argues that crime is a response to the failure of informal social control, caused in turn by a breakdown in social bonds in disorganised neighbourhoods. Stable communities, by contrast, act like villages, building stronger bonds between residents and allowing communities to self-regulate. This has led to hopes – discussed in the previous section – that supporting communities could ultimately reduce demand on the police.

These social ties are central to many subsequent ideas about what makes a strong community. For example, Putnam and others developed ideas of social capital as the ability of people to benefit from their membership of social networks (Coleman, 1988; Putnam, 1995b). At the core of this is the idea that non-monetary resources can provide power and influence. Social capital is a feature of our relations with each other.

Different sociological thinkers give slightly different accounts of what social capital is and how it works. For Bourdieu (1986), social capital describes the benefits which individuals gain as a result of participating in groups, and argued that sociability is essentially constructed for this purpose. Putnam, who famously observed the withering of social ties in modern American life in his book *Bowling alone* (1995a), by contrast, defined social capital as a community level resource, involving 'features of social organisation such as networks, norms, and social trust that facilitate co-ordination and co-operation for mutual benefit' (Putnam, 1995b, p67).

Scholars have also identified different types of social capital. For example, Szreter and Woolcock (2004) distinguish between bonding, bridging and linking capital. Bonding social capital is dense and localised. These are 'strong ties' (Granovetter, 1973), characterised by high levels of intimacy and trust, such as with friends and family. In a community with high levels of bonding capital, residents are more likely to know each other by name and even to be related to other people that live nearby.

Bridging capital, by contrast, is characterised by weak ties and trust, but can connect people across broad social divisions. This can link people who come from different communities and social groups. Bridging capital may have a high predictive power in terms of whether individuals see existing institutions such as the police as legitimate, and therefore feel part of a social order (Szreter, 2002). This echoes the earlier discussion around what supports public confidence in policing. Linking capital is a specific type of bridging capital that links formal organisations beyond the community, such as the police, with the community itself: 'people who are interacting across explicit, formal or institutionalised power or authority gradients in society' (Szreter and Woolcock, 2004, p655). This could describe activities such as police–community engagement, or the connections built through problem-solving; a topic returned to in the next section.

Collective efficacy – a set of processes that allows social control based on weak, rather than strong, ties – is the capacity to undertake collective action to address issues such as crime or disorder. If social capital describes the benefits that can accrue from social bonds, 'collective efficacy' is the capacity to draw on these resources (Sampson, 2002). Collective efficacy theory is a departure from early understandings of the effects of social disorganisation, as it suggests that neighbourhoods can vary widely in social control regardless of residential stability or levels of deprivation – though concentrated disadvantage can affect collective efficacy and therefore lead to higher levels of violence.

Community policing can help generate social capital – particularly of the linking type – through officers making themselves more accessible, and through ensuring representative participation (Scott, 2002). Bridging capital can also be built through facilitating community engagement events that incorporate people from different communities; there is evidence that efforts to co-produce community safety lead to increases in levels of participation and greater knowledge of other people in the area (Singer, 2004). Satisfaction with police can also contribute to informal social control (Silver and Miller, 2004).

However, there are some criticisms of the idea of social capital. As previously discussed, definitions of social capital vary and it can therefore be difficult to identify and measure. In particular, research has struggled to find a consistent relationship between community policing, social capital and collective efficacy. For example, some scholars argue that the process is actually the other way around, and perceptions of police legitimacy might rest on existing levels of social capital (Hawdon, 2008) – so more disorganised and less connected areas have lower levels of police legitimacy, rather than social capital being something that can be improved by good local policing. The NRPP evaluation found no significant effects on informal social control (Tuffin et al, 2006).

It may be that urban communities in the UK do not work in quite the way that studies are assuming. Informal social control is often measured by willingness to intervene, or perceptions of neighbours' willingness to do so. These assessments require some knowledge both of one's neighbours, and of disorder, neither of which can be taken for granted in a world where many of us are much more geographically mobile over the course of our lives (Hipp, 2016).

Direct intervention may no longer be a normal way of dealing with problems; calling the police is much more likely (Gau, 2014). A willingness to intervene may rest on factors such as how present a resident is in their neighbourhood – as discussed earlier, the signal crimes perspective encouraged a focus on 'key individuals' who spent a lot of time in, and had a lot of knowledge of, their local areas. Someone who commutes to work in a different city might feel themselves to have much less knowledge of a neighbourhood and therefore be less willing to participate or intervene. Confidence, communication skills and fear of crime may also have an effect, and fear is often variable according to demographic factors such as age and sex.

Finally, willingness to intervene may be affected by what Kleinhans and Bolt (2014) call 'public familiarity' with neighbours. This describes the everyday social interactions and the weak relationships that develop from these. Neighbours in their study location didn't necessarily want to 'have coffee with each other'; rather, they gained enough information from these limited encounters to recognise and categorise each other. Such 'public familiarity' could later develop into closer ties or trust, but not necessarily – indeed, public familiarity could even develop into mistrust – but it does allow neighbours to be able to understand what to expect from each other. The decline of local facilities such as shops and pubs may be damaging the 'casual public contact' which operates as informal reassurance and makes people feel safe and secure in their neighbourhoods (Barker, 2014, p3059).

A decline in willingness to intervene may mean that informal social control is better demonstrated by a willingness to cooperate with police (Bradford and Jackson, 2016). An effective community may now be better thought of as one where residents feel a responsibility to their neighbourhood and will contact the police in response to crime and disorder, even if they are not prepared to personally intervene to prevent disorder.

This draws on an idea called 'new parochialism' (Carr, 2003). This suggests that we should not think of close social ties and connections with officialdom as separate arenas, as people no longer live like this. The close 'parochial' ties of older types of community have begun to dissolve in modern societies, due to our increased mobility and the capacity of technology to connect us for things like work and study. Carr's study found that residents were not willing to intervene in, for example, disputes between teenagers, calling the police instead. This 'new parochialism' is a combination of private and public control, where residents' desire to intervene is facilitated by public actors such as local politicians and the police.

In a modern urban environment, fostering such 'weak ties' (Granovetter, 1973) may in any case be a better aim than strong social cohesion, as it has the potential to promote open and tolerant communities, which are a better way of organising neighbourhoods in a globalised world than trying to rely on strong ties between friends and family – a return to a way of living that could by definition be quite insular and exclusive (Crawford, 2006).

This is important when we look at what makes an effective community and how officers relate to the neighbourhoods that they police. In particular, it is important when looking at the limits of the police remit, a question to which this chapter will return shortly. If effective communities are those in which residents are more willing to call the police, this means that community-building may not reduce demand in terms of calls for service. Those calls for service are part of the collective efficacy that prevents crime and disorder escalating, makes a community more resilient and self-sustaining, and reduces demand on the police in the longer term, and police willingness to respond to these issues is central to building confidence and legitimacy. Community-building therefore needs to be seen as a long-term investment rather than an instrumental means of reducing the work that neighbourhood officers are asked to take on.

New perspectives on community-building

Given the complexities of modern society, a better way of thinking about strong communities may be through ideas such as resilience. There is a growing literature on community resilience in the sphere of emergency management, where it describes the capacity of a community to cope with 'material shocks'.

Resilience policing is a concept that builds on this existing literature to describe a proposed model of policing that will help police to build community capacity. It encompasses the mechanisms of community engagement that has been discussed in earlier chapters, and the importance of recognising that prevention cannot be a task for the police alone. However, it expands on this, suggesting that one of the core tasks for community policing needs to be building networks that do not centre the police (Mutongwizo et al, 2021).

The key insight of resilience policing is to argue that the police task is often defined too narrowly. This is particularly the case in a contemporary context, where new landscapes of harm are emerging, encompassing everything from environmental disasters, cybercrime, terrorism and economic crisis, to man-made threats. Police, as the service of last resort (and often first resort) are increasingly expected to be the first responders to such situations at a time when resources are steadily being eroded. This requires police to act as 'facilitators/enablers in community capacity-building' (Mutongwizo et al, 2021, p6). Just as Problem-Oriented Policing (POP) called for a shift in the unit of police business from crimes to problems, resilience policing suggests a further shift, from problems to responses, facilitated but not directed by the police.

Some elements of this are emerging already. Earlier chapters discussed PCCs increasingly taking preventative approaches to crime. These include Violence Reduction Units, which often take an explicitly public health approach to countering serious violent crime. Public health approaches step back from the needs of the individual to focus instead on the needs of the public as a whole. Public health approaches to policing may therefore involve paying attention to the structural factors which can affect the likelihood of people being victims of crime, having contact with the police and entering the criminal justice system (Christmas and Srivastava, 2019, p4). Prevention is at the centre of these: preventing the problem occurring in the first place; intervening early when the problem starts to emerge; and managing ongoing problems to reduce harm. While these activities are sometimes beyond the remit of neighbourhood officers, they tie in well with existing understandings of neighbourhood policing and the importance of focusing on problem-solving and partnership-working.

Senior officers have recognised the validity of such approaches, and the Policing Vision 2025 includes a commitment to proactive preventative activity, and building multi-agency neighbourhood projects – including 'fostering a culture shift ... away from a single organisation mentality towards budgeting and service provision based on a whole-system approach, pooling funds where appropriate' (NPCC, 2017, p7).

However, while these approaches are welcome and show promise for the long-term reduction of crime and particularly violence, and the development of resilient communities, there are risks to them as well. The development of this new agenda is in part a result of the severe austerity-led budget cuts instigated following the 2010 general election. These cuts forced a reassessment of assumptions about the purpose and capacities of police forces (HMIC, 2013) and, coupled with changes in demand, prompted a new set of priorities focused around risk, harm and vulnerability (NPCC, 2017). At the same time, decisions about police priorities have moved away from community-driven concerns and towards 'objective' measures of risk such as the Cambridge Crime Harm Index (Sherman et al, 2016; Ashby, 2017).

This presents real dangers to public confidence in policing. The move away from confidence as a priority for the police, towards vulnerability and harm instead, is one that is difficult to counter. However, it is hard to see how broad public support and confidence in policing can be secured if the bulk of police efforts is focused on vulnerable and marginal individuals and groups, most at risk of involvement in crime and disorder (Loader, 2020) – particularly when much of this effort takes place behind closed doors. Public confidence in the police is not based on 'objective' understandings of risk, or on the absence of future crime, but on expressive concerns about social cohesion, local order and the belief that the police share a moral alignment and community values.

Broad, population-level approaches therefore have to be matched by a recognition of the importance of public confidence in policing and a willingness to invest resources in activities that support it. One approach to community-building that has been slowly gaining traction is known as Asset-Based Community Development (ABCD). This approach has the benefit of not just being embedded in the community but in explicitly recognising what it is that a community values.

ABCD is an approach that prioritises understanding the good things within a community – the strengths, assets and resources that already exist. Like resilience policing, this also represents a departure from seeing problems as the core unit of police business, but in a different direction. Most policing models require the identification of deficits: issues identified either through data or through engaging with the community, that then require the police and partners to step in. Strategies that the community may already be using can be overlooked. ABCD instead asks that practitioners audit the community to see what is already present and what is working (Kretzmann and McKnight, 1993), recognising a community's inherent strengths and existing resources.

Asset-based approaches are already being utilised in concert with public health approaches in some areas. For example, in Hawkshill in Glasgow, officers implemented an ABCD approach that they described as 'leading from the back' (Jack et al, 2021). The ABCD approach is a slow one: it involves developing relationships, identifying networks that can contribute (asset mapping), gathering stories of community successes and analysing the reasons for this success.

An asset-based approach can facilitate resilience through building the networks outlined earlier. It can support public health approaches by connecting public agencies with community groups and residents. From a police point of view, it also has the advantage of embedding officers within the community and actively asking members of that community about the things that they value and the strengths of their local neighbourhood (Mathie and Cunningham, 2003). This makes ABCD a particularly valuable potential strategy for neighbourhood police officers as it actively facilitates the demonstration of moral alignment and guardianship of a local area, it incorporates the mechanisms of neighbourhood policing – community engagement, visibility, and where appropriate, problem-solving – while building the kind of social capital and collective efficacy that serves a preventative purpose.

Such community-building strategies attempt to reach far upstream of the traditional remit of the police. While not directly building community capacity, they certainly aim to contribute to facilitating its growth. As Barnes and Eagle (2007, p170) put it, perhaps 'it is not the role of the police to create social capital but to allow the space for it to flourish by providing a sense of security where connections can be made'. The extent to which neighbourhood policing should take on this role, however, remains a topic of debate, and the next section looks at whether community-building should even be part of the neighbourhood policing remit.

The limits of the police role

The question of what policing should be for, and what should be its limits, is one that recurs in policy and throughout this book. Some argue that policing has expanded its remit too far, particularly during the late 1990s and 2000s. This critique comes despite the shedding of ancillary tasks in the 1990s and the pluralisation of many policing roles.

The argument that the police role has become too wide rests on the push towards neighbourhood policing and the move towards preventative police work. Some examples of areas in which the policing mandate may have become too wide include police engaging in offender management, which critics argue involves them acting as probation officers and social workers (Millie, 2013); officers being embedded in schools; engaging in disaster management, or acting as stewards or event security. Millie argues for a more narrow conception of policing, and the refocusing of the core policing task. From this perspective, the task of community-building falls well outside the police remit and should be handed back to those better qualified and explicitly trained for such jobs – even if this means the shrinking of the police workforce to match.

However, at a time when many partners have also come under severe budgetary pressures, it is not clear whether or how the police can step back (Millie, 2013, p149). Some forces have tried to limit their role. Humberside Police, for example, were awarded an 'outstanding' grade by Her Majesty's Inspectorate of Constabulary and Fire and Rescue Services in six of nine areas in 2022 – just five years after the force found itself in 'special measures'. The turnaround was in part ascribed to several measures taken by senior officers to limit the activities of officers that went beyond an identified police remit. For example, a new approach called Right Care, Right Person aimed to ensure that those in mental health crisis were no longer accompanied by a police officer to hospital as a matter of course, saving over 1,000 police hours a month (Jacques, 2022). However, even in Humberside, the Inspectorate congratulated the force on its neighbourhood model which invested considerable time in partnerships and early intervention with children and young people.

The expansion in numbers during the Labour government that Millie notes was largely in neighbourhood officers. Given the more recent downturn in public confidence (Police Foundation, 2022), and the subtle change in political rhetoric towards defending a front-line presence in communities, it is hard to see many political or policing benefits in further narrowing the police mandate. Doing so may also present many difficulties, given the increasing interdependence of public sector organisations on the ground.

Some have argued that the organisational changes wrought by austerity and changing demand are more permanent: 'the police have become more at a distance, more impersonal and formal, less direct, and more decontextualised' (Terpstra et al, 2019, p340). A shift to such 'abstract policing' would be a fundamental departure from the model required for community-building.

The idea of abstract police discussed by Terpstra et al has two main aspects: internal and external relations. Internal relations refers to the outcome of reorganisations within forces for reasons of flexibility and capacity (Terpstra et al, 2019, p343). This leads to a loss of personal contact and an increasing reliance on formalised procedures to deal with issues that could have been resolved better – and certainly more quickly – through informal channels or the use of local knowledge; just as seen in Chapter 7 when problems emerge with external partnerships. Externally, the authors found a similar move away from connection between officers and citizens, and with external partners, in part to deal with increased demand. This included a shift to reporting minor crimes online, and the loss of police stations. Such shifts not only distance police officers from citizens, but limit the flow of intelligence and the richness of the stories to which officers have access.

Abstract policing as a model is an important way of understanding the directions in which policing can turn when an understanding of the value of connection is lost. However, while many of the driving forces behind abstract policing as a phenomenon are identifiable on a broader stage, it is not clear that they represent an irresistible momentum.

For example, it is undoubtedly true that some forms of increasing reliance on data can actively distance the police from the communities they serve: for example, the last section argued that the move towards harm metrics can damage confidence in the longer term as there is no systematic method within crime harm models of including legitimacy considerations. However, data collection and intelligence gathering does not have to be an abstracting process. As seen in Chapter 6, the incorporation of intelligence and crime data into community-led models of problem-solving is an important element of effective neighbourhood policing.

There is also evidence that the direction of travel is not inevitably towards the abstract. For example, the issuance of neighbourhood policing guidelines with explicit reference to empowering communities to encourage them 'to look after themselves without the support of the police' (CoP, 2018c, p9) suggests that community-building may yet emerge as an important new direction in neighbourhood policing.

Policing is both the coercive arm of the state, and a symbolic representative of the state as a political entity, requiring a political claim for legitimacy. In the UK, this claim is made in the particular terms of 'policing by consent', as discussed in Chapter 2. This tension is therefore not a cycle so much as a constant tension between two competing imperatives, both integral to the nature of policing. Austerity required UK police to re-examine their core purposes in a context of limited budgets. This exercise was therefore designed to make choices that excluded purposes that were difficult to quantify – those of legitimation. But the current crisis of legitimacy is requiring forces to return to these questions and to renew their commitment to longer-term goals.

Neighbourhood policing needs to be seen over the long term. Community-building is a valuable activity for policing precisely because it can reduce demand on the police seen over years rather than weeks or months; and it complements the other mechanisms through which confidence is supported. This work, through proactive engagement, building networks and supporting partners, underpins confidence and the capacity of communities to help themselves – entirely in the interests of the police when seen from this longer-term perspective. Expectations of the police may well be limitless, but are much more manageable when the police are just one node in a wider nexus of strong communities and capable partners.

Summary

The idea that neighbourhood policing could contribute to building strong, resilient communities was a central part of the original philosophy that underpinned its place in government policy. It was less explicitly incorporated into the Neighbourhood Policing Programme itself, however, and it was always challenged by those who believed in a narrower police task.

Austerity then contributed to the erosion of this. By forcing forces to reconsider the purpose of policing in a budget-driven framework, the purposes of policing were inevitably recalibrated around what could be measured, and what fitted with the values of police forces rather than the values of communities. Thus neighbourhood policing now serves many purposes, some of which actively crowd out its capacity to serve its original purpose of increasing confidence.

However, the damage to confidence and legitimacy that has followed is leading to a revitalisation of neighbourhood policing as a vehicle for increasing public confidence. Meanwhile, many forces are taking a longer view of the challenges facing them and the need to engage in preventative work, in concert with partners, to address some of the more complex issues – such as violence – by tackling their root causes.

There is a lot of evidence around the effects that policing can have on communities; in particular there have been a number of studies on the relationship between community policing and social capital and collective efficacy. However, this relationship is not straightforward. One question is whether we are certain about what a strong community looks like and how it should behave. If strong communities in a modern urban environment express their willingness to intervene by calling the police, this has implications for managing demand and the distribution of resources: while strong and resilient communities reduce demand in the long term, in the short term successful neighbourhood teams may find themselves in more demand than previously.

This is particularly the case should forces decide to take a longer view. Adopting a long-term perspective on police activity, whether this is through building resilience, or public health approaches, or through asset-based activities, requires that officers become facilitators, and spend considerable time on activities that, on the face of it, may seem barely related to crime and disorder. These approaches all have another element in common, which is that the police are not necessarily central to them, but are one node in a wider network. This may require a substantial change in officer understandings of their role. It may also require new skills.

However, all of these approaches have substantial potential benefits if they are approached with public confidence in mind. All of the key elements of good neighbourhood policing – community engagement, visibility, problem-solving and partnership work – are effectively incorporated into these community-building approaches, in ways that demonstrate guardianship, a concern for social order and a concern for the elements of procedural justice, such as voice, respect and trustworthiness.

Some have argued that these tasks are – and should be – beyond the police. These arguments were brought into sharp relief by the challenges posed by steep budget cuts, and continue to resonate given below-inflation funding settlements. The recalibration of the police mission which was mandated by these cuts saw a much greater focus on harm and vulnerability and the disappearance of confidence as a target. Some reorganisations profoundly damaged the capacity of forces to maintain the informal relationships on which co-working depended, even internally. However, it is not clear that the development of 'abstract' policing is inevitable, and the crisis of confidence and legitimacy that has emerged in recent years is forcing senior officers to once again reconsider the importance of work that explicitly focuses on building confidence and legitimacy – concrete, contextualised policing that is embedded in communities and seeks to strengthen them in the long term.

Resources will continue to be a constraint on any attempt to include community-building as a purpose of policing, or to return to confidence as the core purpose of neighbourhood policing. But, as we have seen, resilient communities can reduce long-term demand on policing, and build confidence, creating a virtuous circle with real and measurable benefits to police forces, to their officers, and to the communities they serve.

Questions for further consideration

1. What are the limits of policing? Should community-building be part of that remit?
2. How inevitable do you think is the move towards more abstract policing models?

Further reading
Kretzmann, J. and McKnight, J. 1993. *Building communities from the inside out: A path toward finding and mobilizing a community's assets*. Chicago: The Asset-Based Community Development Institute.

Mathie, A. and Cunningham, G. 2003. *From clients to citizens: Asset-based community development as a strategy for community-driven development.* Development in Practice, 13(5): 474–486.

Putnam, R.D. 2000. *Bowling alone: The collapse and revival of American community.* New York and London: Simon & Schuster.

Terpstra, J., Salet, R. and Fyfe, N.R. (eds). 2022. *The abstract police: Critical reflections on contemporary change in police organisations.* Den Haag: Eleven International Publishing.

9

Themes and future directions

Introduction

Visibility, community engagement and problem-solving remain central to good neighbourhood policing. This book has added the importance of good partnerships and the possibilities of building strong communities. All of these must rest on a solid understanding of the context in which neighbourhood policing arose and the evidence on which it was based; and an understanding of what police legitimacy and public confidence in policing consist of.

This final chapter draws out some of these themes further. It begins by exploring the importance of the political and policy landscape in establishing the context within which neighbourhood policing work takes place. It argues that despite limited short-term grounds for optimism, and below-inflation funding settlements, there may be longer-term reasons to be cheerful. In particular, the establishment of Police and Crime Commissioners (PCCs) has facilitated a range of work which has itself altered the conditions in which policing strategies are made; and the possibility of a change of government in the next several years may also enhance that environment.

This strategic level of governance is also crucial for neighbourhood policing. Recent years have seen something of a renaissance in neighbourhood policing and the seriousness with which these tasks are addressed, thanks to the development of College of Policing (CoP) guidelines (2018b) and the incorporation of community policing as part of the Policing Education Qualifcations Framework (PEQF) curriculum. However, confidence has not returned to its previous centrality as a policing purpose, and this seems unlikely in the current context. This means that the onus is on forces and on neighbourhood officers themselves to ensure that confidence is kept as a driving force behind neighbourhood policing activity.

Likewise, forces and neighbourhood officers can do little to affect the tension that exists between law enforcement and legitimation in policing; nor the cyclical nature by which this comes to public attention. However, they can remain conscious of it. This third theme identifies some areas in which this tension can manifest itself and some hidden dangers in trying to reconcile them.

Finally, the chapter re-examines the central role that relationships play in neighbourhood policing, through making police accessible and visible, to engaging with the community, solving problems and working with partners.

The last chapter in particular underlined how these relationships can form the basis of a more ambitious remit for neighbourhood work: helping to build stronger, more resilient communities.

Neighbourhood policing is a model with enduring power to support public confidence in policing, and one that deserves to be taken seriously and studied carefully. This chapter concludes that there are grounds for optimism for its future, so long as officers and forces remember its central purpose.

Politics and policy landscapes

The first of the themes that have been traced through this book is the importance of the political landscape to operational policing. Many officers would prefer not to think too deeply about politics in their daily work – but politics undoubtedly thinks about them. Notwithstanding the operational independence of the police, and the strategic independence of PCCs, police budgets remain largely dependent upon central funding, which, when cut, force priority-setting strategies that often marginalise the long-term and preventative work in which neighbourhood policing teams specialise, and which supports public confidence and police legitimacy.

A political and policy environment that prioritises public confidence in policing encourages the flourishing of good neighbourhood policing. This was demonstrated in the 2000s with the establishment of the original Neighbourhood Policing Programme, and the ring-fencing of funding for Police Community Support Officers. By contrast, an ideological outlook in government under which the public sector is regarded as over-large, and encroaching too much into people's lives, will likely see rhetorical support for neighbourhood policing dwindle in favour of a more limited police mission.

However, neighbourhood policing is also broadly popular, and politicians from all ideological persuasions need to get re-elected. Despite a relatively hostile environment, therefore, neighbourhood policing continues to operate in most forces, albeit often underfunded, overworked and poorly protected. The announcement of an 'uplift' of 20,000 officers offered some relief to overstretched forces and the possibility of restocking some denuded neighbourhood teams. Moreover, the CoP's 2018 Neighbourhood Policing Guidelines, prompted by the critical 2017 Her Majesty's Inspectorate of Constabulary report, underlined the importance of neighbourhood policing as a central activity – 'the "cornerstone" of British policing'.

This has unfortunately not yet been accompanied by a return to confidence as the central purpose of neighbourhood policing. This means that, despite any increase of officers to neighbourhood policing teams, there is a risk that their remit may be too wide, meeting broader 'business' needs rather than core tasks of being visible, engaging with the community and solving problems. A recognition that neighbourhood work needs to be ring-fenced, and focused on long-term, preventative work, with substantial partnership and community-building functions, may be necessary for any genuine renaissance of neighbourhood policing in the UK.

It is difficult at the time of writing to discern a clear position from the current government on neighbourhood policing. There were three prime ministers, three different home secretaries and four ministers of state for policing over the course of a turbulent 2022 – not ideal circumstances for the development of coherent and well-directed policing policy. The Beating Crime Plan, released in 2021 under Boris Johnson, focuses largely on serious crime and violence, and refers to neighbourhood policing only in terms of making local teams more accessible online (Home Office, 2021).

More hopefully, the Labour Party is currently committing to tackling the 'root causes' of community issues, and to higher police numbers (Labour Party, 2022). However, some details of these policies are currently lacking. In its early years of opposition, the Labour Party commissioned an independent report on the future of policing, led by Lord Stevens. The Commission's report is explicit that it sees the remit of the police as a wide one: 'The police are not simply crime fighters. Their civic purpose is focused on improving safety and well-being within communities and promoting measures to prevent crime, harm and disorder' (Stevens, 2013, p14). This suggests the possibility that a future Labour government might take a different approach to the role of the police. However, as with the Conservative Party, leadership changes mean that policies laid out in earlier years may no longer be relevant to future plans.

In the meantime there are pragmatic causes for optimism for neighbourhood policing. PCCs are already in post, and are able to set strategic goals and bid for funding. As directly elected officials, PCCs need to respond to public concerns; which are often, as seen in earlier chapters, around low-level issues such as anti-social behaviour. As a result of this, anti-social behaviour has been highlighted as a key priority in all police and crime plans in England and Wales, according to the Association of Police and Crime Commissioners (APCC, 2021). On the ground, PCCs are undertaking a range of work that reflects this wider understanding of the role of policing, including prevention work, collaboration with partners to reduce demand, and to address community concerns. PCCs are also often found supporting neighbourhood work with the rhetoric (and sometimes the organisational focus) that can be missing nationally.

Overall, then, if the immediate outlook is limited, there is long-term promise for neighbourhood policing from a policy standpoint. Many PCCs do substantial work in the area; the Labour Party is broadly committed to preventative work and an increase in police numbers, and even under sustained assault from budget cuts, the outline of a neighbourhood policing model is still recognisable in most forces. Most hopefully from a pragmatic position is the embedding of community policing in the curriculum of the PEQF, and the issuing of neighbourhood guidelines from the CoP. Though neither are perfect, it is these that will continue to embed the organisational philosophy that can sustain neighbourhood work through any difficult days ahead; and the chapter turns to these next.

The purpose of policing

The last section outlined in depth the extent to which New Labour's policy programme set the scene for the development and embedding of neighbourhood policing, and in more recent years how the challenges to it have emerged from national decisions on funding. We can see how this has affected force decisions on the allocation of scarce resources, and how a shift away from confidence as the core purpose of neighbourhood policing towards other business needs can undermine neighbourhood work in practice. The second theme that can be identified is therefore the importance of strategic police priorities, both at force level and nationally.

The austerity-driven obligation to review strategic force priorities led to a national shift towards a greater focus on vulnerability and harm, and new metrics to measure the latter. This change in focus had clear effects on the mechanisms of neighbourhood policing that drive confidence. For example, while focusing patrols in crime hot spots demonstrably reduces crime, it does so at a cost if forces remove all police presence from areas with relatively lower crime. If forces withdraw – deliberately or as an unforeseen consequence of other decisions – from community engagement activities, or they lose their Police Community Support Officers, then confidence is likely to be damaged in the longer term regardless of the benefits for the force in 'refocusing' these assets. If problems important to local communities are left unresolved because police are concentrating resources on high-harm issues, then perceptions of effectiveness will be damaged as well as trust. All of these are long-term issues for policing that will have to be addressed eventually.

Budget cuts have also had serious effects on other elements of neighbourhood policing too – such as partnerships and community-building. Refocusing the police mission on vulnerability and harm can support some kinds of multi-agency partnerships – indeed, partners are vital for police to address vulnerability effectively – but prioritising these to the exclusion of community issues can damage them. This can happen for example through the abstraction of neighbourhood officers, which undermines the building of stable, long-term relationships between individuals that make partnerships work effectively. Effective partnerships rest on the informal trust and strong relationships that is built by experienced officers having the time to build them. Established neighbourhood teams can accrue vital local knowledge and become part of an extensive network that cannot be replaced elsewhere in the force structure by officers responding to incidents.

Similarly, a focus on vulnerability and harm can lead to forces targeting their limited resources to avoid 'wasting' officers' time on low-level issues in low-crime neighbourhoods. It can also lead them to think about problems in terms of marginal individuals at risk of engaging with the criminal justice system, rather than community concerns; and to trust police data over the issues raised by residents. Yet it is the process of seeking out those concerns, of being present in communities, and of thinking of places in the round, that supports public confidence in the police. This in turn allows the police to become one node in a wider network that can help develop communities to become more resilient and reduce longer-term demand.

However, there have been some major changes in recent years that offer some optimism for the future of neighbourhood policing. Her Majesty's Inspectorate of Constabulary's 2016 report on police effectiveness did more than just raise the alarm over the state of neighbourhood policing across the country; it laid down basic expectations for it. In particular it called for the CoP to issue national guidance on the essential elements of neighbourhood policing. This included public engagement, problem-solving, partnerships and patrolling, all with a preventative function. It underlined the importance of neighbourhood policing to building trust and confidence, and reiterated that neighbourhood policing is a cost-effective approach: problem-solving and crime prevention is nearly always cheaper than investigating crimes after they have taken place.

The development of the CoP's guidelines built on this framework, establishing foundations for neighbourhood policing as a model. This book has identified some concerns with the guidelines, which depart from the original philosophy of neighbourhood policing in three main ways: targeting rather than universalism; the demotion of public confidence in policing as a central purpose of neighbourhood work; and the focus on reflecting existing changes to practice. The most important of these is the receding of confidence as a purpose, to become just one priority at the bottom of a list of four desired outcomes, along with protecting local neighbourhoods, safeguarding the vulnerable, and managing and diverting offenders (CoP, 2018a, p3). However, notwithstanding these concerns, the new guidelines are comprehensive and evidence-based, and clearly outline effective ways for officers to implement the core mechanisms of good neighbourhood work. As such they are an excellent framework for neighbourhood policing in practice – particularly if forces and officers themselves are prepared to see public confidence as the central purpose of the neighbourhood policing model.

Finally, the PEQF curriculum sought to enshrine an understanding of community policing as a model in the basic education of all police officers.

Notwithstanding potential changes to police education in the future, the first wave of PEQF entrants are now entering the police through the uplift, and many more will follow. Community policing is only one area of teaching; the extensive curriculum ensures new officers also learn police powers, road policing, and how to arrest and detain, among a broad range of skills. Nevertheless, the presence of community policing in this compulsory curriculum is enormously important to the development of effective neighbourhood officers, and as a recognition of the permanence of neighbourhood policing as a feature of British policing.

Law enforcement and legitimacy

One of the reasons that the continuation of neighbourhood policing is so vital is the recurrent crises in police legitimacy. Recent global and local events have put a spotlight on police legitimacy once again. The persistent need to think about how we legitimate policing as the coercive arm of the state, and the related importance of sustaining public confidence in policing, are themes that run throughout this book. The third theme examined is therefore the tension between the law enforcement imperative of policing, and the need to legitimate that coercive power.

Visibility and foot patrol support confidence, but to do so, they need to be undertaken with confidence in mind. If they are done primarily for the purposes of law enforcement, they can actively damage confidence, through aggressive interactions and arrests. Thus police must be part of the 'warp and weft that [holds] a community together' (O'Reilly, 2023); they need to patrol with the purpose of confidence-building in mind – even as their purpose is to reassure residents of their security through the latent threat of coercive force.

This tension is a constant one, and can also be seen in the processes of engaging with communities and problem-solving. What communities often demand from police is a coercive response to their problems; and forces can be criticised extensively for failing to 'crack down' on problems such as anti-social behaviour and drug-dealing. Yet the roots and the solutions to such problems often lie not in enforcement but persuasion and partnership working, based on trust and an understanding that the causes of such problems are found far upstream. It is engagement itself that can reassure communities that they have a voice and are heard when their problems are complex and long term, and 'enforcement' solutions are either disproportionate, beyond the police remit, or simply impracticable given resource or other constraints.

Coercive law enforcement approaches can also undermine the trust that is central to building good partnerships and building good communities. Chapter 7 explored the reality that organisational values can come into conflict in multi-agency partnerships, and in particular that organisations that see themselves as focused on the welfare of offenders can mistrust the police if they are seen to be taking a primarily enforcement-focused approach. Moreover, a community-building approach requires the police to be one node in a network of engagement, requiring the establishment of trust-based relationships.

However, the language of 'crackdowns' can be appealing to residents, while welfare-based approaches can lead to residents feeling the crime and disorder that they are experiencing is not taken sufficiently seriously. Thus the language of policy matters, and the relative weight given to coercion versus legitimacy, to how policing is experienced by partners and residents as well as offenders. Penal populism is popular for a reason. And even for Labour politicians, as Blair discovered in the mid-1990s, 'law and order' is often a core issue for voters in swing seats. Basic statecraft necessitates that politicians respond to the things that matter to their voters – it is what supports their democratic legitimacy.

As such, policing and politics have to recognise and address both the experience of crime and disorder in neighbourhoods and the causes of that crime: to listen to residents and respond to their issues, even when minor, using coercive power when required; but also to take the time to build relationships, offer more than crusading rhetoric, and to understand and work with others to tackle the complex, multifaceted and often structural issues that cause that crime and disorder. The next section explores those relationships as the final major theme identified in this book.

Relationships and connections

The final theme that has emerged over the course of this book is the centrality to policing of relationships. To police a neighbourhood is not simply to apply a treatment (Wood et al, 2014). It is to become part of a community, in a complex set of relations. The neighbourhood police officer is a guardian by virtue of being the formal representative of the coercive weight of the law, while confidence in that officer rests on their capacity to build day-to-day relationships resting on informality and trust.

It is these relationships that are central to neighbourhood policing. Trust and confidence is affective, not instrumental. Residents want to feel connected, safe, and part of a community and a wider society. They want to belong, and insecurity, incivility and fear of crime all wear away at that sense of belonging. Good neighbourhood policing can signal to residents that they belong; they are safe; their voices are heard, and their beliefs, values and opinions count. An understanding that what counts for communities is locally variable is at the centre of this.

Visible policing is therefore more than a presence in a community: it is about being accessible and familiar as well. A named set of officers, with a regular, long-term presence in a neighbourhood, can begin to build relationships with ordinary residents as well as those at risk of becoming victims or offenders, and can build deep local knowledge and resilient sources of intelligence over months and years.

A permanent physical presence in a neighbourhood through police stations or their equivalent was traditionally the basis of that accessibility. Nothing can really replace the capacity to go and speak to a known police officer, face-to-face, in terms of building authentic relationships. In the absence of a permanent physical presence, regular meetings – even if poorly attended – are the next best thing. These are not about filling a hall on every occasion with engaged residents (indeed, this can often signal serious problems). Rather, they are about establishing conduits through which residents can access police support when they need it. Engagement with local councillors, establishing volunteer community chairs or organising ward panels along the lines of those operating in London are all ways of enhancing that conduit.

Ongoing public meetings have benefits for relationship-building that go beyond their formal processes. Unlike street surgeries, which can reach people, but by their nature are roving and will infrequently visit the same area, public meetings with their regularity can provide authentic connection and certainty. Residents know that, even if they don't attend, the meetings will be there when they need them. And meetings themselves provide not just familiarity and accessibility, but liminal space on their edges for informal conversations that residents might be shy of beginning publicly. These face-to-face engagements are sites where affective relationships can begin and can be maintained.

Effective community engagement therefore needs to be seen as activity that builds relationships, not just as a means of talking at a community. Good communications strategies are important, but should be seen in terms of reflecting the issues that communities have raised: communication cannot replace authentic engagement but can only build on it. Problem-solving, similarly, requires the genuine buy-in of local residents; data alone will do little to address subjective fear of crime if it leads to police focusing on volume crimes, or, indeed, high-harm crimes, to the exclusion of low-level issues that matter more to communities.

Addressing residents' problems effectively depends on building partnerships. These, as previously discussed, are all about the power of relationships to engender trust, and to allow officers at times to bypass the formal structures that their power depends on. Even resolving problems that stem from conflicts over fundamental values can be facilitated by a strong network of relationships; allowing officers to recognise what these different values are and how they might come into conflict.

Finally, for neighbourhood policing to be effective in building strong communities, officers have to be prepared to focus on the web of relationships and connections that extend beyond their own reach. Officers have the power to build bridging and linking capital through their neighbourhood activities, like community engagement and problem-solving, and to increase collective efficacy. But to go further upstream, policing will increasingly need to see itself as just one element in a wider network of formal and informal relationships between community groups, public sector agencies and others. Moving policing outside the centre – at times, even being marginal to events that officers have facilitated – may be a new challenge, but it is one with huge potential for the success of local communities, and by extension, of neighbourhood teams in supporting public confidence in policing.

Summary

One of the key observations of the *Strategic review of policing* recently undertaken by the Police Foundation was that confidence was beginning to fall. The annual *State of policing* report also noted that policing capacity had suffered due to years of underfunding (HMICFRS, 2022). With the current uplift of 20,000 officers, there exists an opportunity to 'reset' policing and to review strategic priorities. However, this requires decisions to be made about how to properly measure police success and to shape strategic priorities in the future. Risk, harm and performance are likely to remain part of that: however, should they continue to dominate, the drop in confidence may be more difficult to turn around.

Nevertheless, the outlook for neighbourhood policing is promising. The need to balance law enforcement with legitimation has largely been institutionalised, as has neighbourhood policing as a model. PCCs are pioneering public health approaches, and forces are looking to extend their preventative capacity. The CoP's guidelines are clear, effective and evidence-based, and community policing principles are included in most new officers' training.

For this optimism to be well-placed, officers and forces need to remember that the central role of neighbourhood policing is to support public confidence in policing. The model may well be able to support other strategic aims; however, if it loses its capacity to support confidence it is neighbourhood policing in name only. Neighbourhood policing also needs to be locally determined. It is not sufficient to determine at force level what local priorities should be, such as vulnerability, harm or crime indexes, and then 'do the right thing' – processes need to be in place to work with residents to determine what the right things are. It is this work itself that supports confidence and has the potential to support strong communities as well.

References

ACPO (Association of Chief Police Officers). 2006. *Practice advice on professionalising the business of neighbourhood policing.* London: ACPO.

Alderson, J.C. 1979. *Policing freedom: A commentary on the dilemmas of policing in western democracies.* Estover: Macdonald and Evans.

Almandras, S., Ward, P., Woodhouse, J. and Ares, E. 2010. *Police reform and social responsibility bill.* London: House of Commons Library. Available at https://researchbriefings.files.parliament.uk/documents/RP10-81/RP10-81.pdf [Accessed 7 October 2017].

APCC (Association of Police and Crime Commissioners). 2021. *Ten years of PCCs making a difference: Anti-social behaviour – making communities safer.* Available at https://www.apccs.police.uk/ten-years-of-pccs-making-a-difference/anti-social-behaviour-making-communities-safer/ [Accessed 9 November 2022].

APCC and NPCC (Association of Police and Crime Commissioners and National Police Chiefs' Council). 2016. *Policing vision 2025.* Available at https://www.npcc.police.uk/documents/Policing%20Vision.pdf [Accessed 30 August 2017].

Ariel, B., Weinborn, C. and Sherman, L.W. 2016. 'Soft' policing at hot spots—do police community support officers work? A randomized controlled trial. *Journal of Experimental Criminology*, 12(3): 277–317.

Ashby, M.P. 2017. Comparing methods for measuring crime harm/severity. *Policing: A Journal of Policy and Practice*, 12(4): 439–454.

ASU (Arizona State University) Center for Problem-Oriented Policing. nd. *The SARA model.* Available at https://popcenter.asu.edu/content/sara-model-0 [Accessed 19 December 2021].

Audit Commission. 1996. *Streetwise: Effective police patrol.* London: HMSO.

Bangs, M. 2016. *Research outputs: Developing a Crime Severity Score for England and Wales using data on crimes recorded by the police.* Available at https://www.ons.gov.uk/peoplepopulationandcommunity/crimeandjustice/articles/researchoutputsdevelopingacrimeseverityscoreforenglandandwalesusingdataoncrimesrecordedbythepolice/2016-11-29 [Accessed 16 July 2019].

Barker, A. 2014. Communicating security? Policing urban spaces and control signals. *Urban Studies*, 51(14): 3046–3061.

Barnes, I. and Eagle, T. 2007. The role of community engagement in neighbourhood policing. *Policing: A Journal of Policy and Practice*, 1(2): 161–172.

Bayley, D. 1988. Community policing: A report from the devil's advocate. In J.R. Greene and S.D. Mastrofski (eds) *Community policing: Rhetoric or reality.* New York: Praeger, pp225–238.

Bennett, T. 1991. The effectiveness of a police-initiated fear-reducing strategy. *The British Journal of Criminology*, 31(1): 1–14.

Bittner, E. 2005. Florence Nightingale in pursuit of Willie Hutton: A theory of the police. In: T. Newburn (ed) *Policing: Key readings*. Cullompton: Willan Publishing, pp150–172.

Blair, G., Weinstein, J.M., Christia, F., Arias, E., Badran, E., Blair, R.A., Cheema, A., Farooqui, A., Fetzer, T., Grossman, G. and Haim, D. 2021. Community policing does not build citizen trust in police or reduce crime in the Global South. *Science*, 374(6571): eabd3446.

Bland, M., Leggetter, M., Cestaro, D. and Sebire, J. 2021. Fifteen minutes per day keeps the violence away: A crossover randomised controlled trial on the impact of foot patrols on serious violence in large hot spot areas. *Cambridge Journal of Evidence-Based Policing*, 5(3): 93–118.

BMG Research. 2019. *Public perceptions of policing in England and Wales 2018*. Available at https://www.bmgresearch.co.uk//wp-content/uploads/2019/01/1578-HMICFRS-Public-Perceptions-of-Policing-2018_FINAL.pdf [Accessed 12 October 2019].

Bochel, C., Bochel, H., Somerville, P. and Worley, C. 2008. Marginalised or enabled voices? 'User participation' in policy and practice. *Social Policy and Society*, 7(2): 201–210.

Borovec, K., Balgač, I. and Mraović, I.C. 2019. Police visibility as an influencing factor on citizens' perception of safety. *Journal of Criminal Justice and Security*, 2: 135–160.

Borrion, H., Ekblom, P., Alrajeh, D., Borrion, A.L., Keane, A., Koch, D., Mitchener-Nissen, T. and Toubaline, S. 2020. The problem with crime problem-solving: Towards a second generation POP? *The British Journal of Criminology*, 60(1): 219–240.

Bottoms, A. and Tankebe, J. 2012. Beyond procedural justice: A dialogic approach to legitimacy in criminal justice. *Journal of Criminal Law and Criminology*, 102(1): 119–170.

Bourdieu, P. 1986. The forms of capital. In J.G. Richardson (ed) *Handbook of theory and research for the sociology of education*. New York: Greenwood, pp241–258.

Bradford, B. 2011. Convergence, not divergence? Trends and trajectories in public contact and confidence in the police. *British Journal of Criminology*, 51(1): 179–200.

Bradford, B. 2014. Policing and social identity: Procedural justice, inclusion and cooperation between police and public. *Policing and Society*, 24(1): 22–43.

Bradford, B. and Jackson, J. 2010. Trust and confidence in the police: A conceptual review. *SSRN Journal*. Available at https://doi.org/10.2139/ssrn.1684508 [Accessed 10 May 2019].

Bradford, B. and Jackson, J. 2016. Cooperating with the police as an act of social control: Trust and neighbourhood concerns as predictors of public assistance. *Nordisk Politiforskning*, 3(2): 111–131.

Bradford, B., Jackson, J., Hough, M. and Farrall, S. 2009a. Trust and confidence in criminal justice: A review of the British research literature. In A. Jokinen, E. Ruuskanen, M. Yordanova, D. Markov and M. Ilcheva (eds) *Review of need: Indicators of public confidence in criminal justice*. Available at https://papers.ssrn.com/sol3/papers.cfm?abstract_id=1303567 [Accessed 10 May 2019].

Bradford, B., Jackson, J. and Stanko, E.A. 2009b. Contact and confidence: Revisiting the impact of public encounters with the police. *Policing and Society*, 19(1): 20–46.

Bradford, B., Murphy, K. and Jackson, J. 2014. Officers as mirrors: Policing, procedural justice and the (re) production of social identity. *British Journal of Criminology*, 54(4): 527–550.

Bradford, B., Topping, J., Martin, R. and Jackson, J. 2018. Can diversity promote trust? Neighbourhood context and trust in the police in Northern Ireland. *Policing and Society*: 1–20. https://doi.org/10.1080/10439463.2018.1479409

Bradley, R. 1998. *Public expectations and perceptions of policing*. Police research series, paper 96. London: Home Office Policing and Reducing Crime Unit, Research, Development and Statistics Directorate.

Braga, A.A. 2007. Effects of hot spots policing on crime. *Campbell Systematic Reviews*, 3(1): 1–36.

Braga, A.A. and Weisburd, D. 2006. Problem-oriented policing: The disconnect between principles and practice. In D. Weisburd and A.A. Braga (eds) *Police innovation: Contrasting perspectives*. Cambridge: Cambridge University Press, pp133–154.

Braga, A.A., and Bond, B.J. 2008. Policing crime and disorder hot spots: A randomized controlled trial. *Criminology*, 46(3): 577–607.

Braga, A., Papachristos, A. and Hureau, D. 2012. Hot spots policing effects on crime. *Campbell Systematic Reviews*, 8(8): 1–96.

Braga, A.A., Turchan, B.S., Papachristos, A.V. and Hureau, D.M. 2019. Hot spots policing and crime reduction: An update of an ongoing systematic review and meta-analysis. *Journal of Experimental Criminology*, 15(3): 289–311.

Braverman, S. 2022. Suella Braverman at the APCC and NPCC Partnership Summit. Speech. 9 November. Available at https://www.gov.uk/government/speeches/suella-braverman-at-the-apcc-and-npcc-partnership-summit [Accessed 9 November 2022].

Brewer, R. 2013. Enhancing crime control partnerships across government: Examining the role of trust and social capital on American and Australian waterfronts. *Police Quarterly*, 16(4): 371–394.

Brownlee, I. 1998. New Labour – new penology? Punitive rhetoric and the limits of managerialism in criminal justice policy. *Journal of Law and Society*, 25(3): 313–335.

Brunger, M. 2014. Exploring the myth of the bobby and the intrusion of the state into social space. *International Journal for the Semiotics of Law-Revue internationale de Sémiotique juridique*, 27(1): 121–134.

Bull, D. and Stratta, E. 1994. Police community consultation: An examination of its practice in selected constabularies in England and New South Wales, Australia. *Australian and New Zealand Journal of Criminology*, 27(3): 237–249.

Buller, J. and James, T.S. 2012. Statecraft and the assessment of national political leaders: The case of New Labour and Tony Blair. *The British Journal of Politics and International Relations*, 14(4): 534–555.

Bullock, K. 2010. Generating and using community intelligence: The case of neighbourhood policing. *International Journal of Police Science and Management*, 12(1): 1–11.

Bullock, K. 2014. *Citizens, community and crime control*. Basingstoke: Palgrave Macmillan.

Bullock, K. 2018. The police use of social media: Transformation or normalisation? *Social Policy and Society*, 17(2): 245–258.

Bullock, K. and Tilley, N. 2009. Born to fail? Policing, reform and neighbourhood problem solving. *The Police Journal*, 82(2): 117–133.

Bullock, K. and Leeney, D. 2013. Participation, 'responsivity' and accountability in neighbourhood policing. *Criminology and Criminal Justice*, 13(2): 199–214.

Bullock, K. and Sindall, K. 2014. Examining the nature and extent of public participation in neighbourhood policing. *Policing and Society*, 24(4): 385–404.

Bullock, K., Sidebottom, A., Armitage, R., Ashby, M.P., Clemmow, C., Kirby, S., Laycock, G. and Tilley, N. 2021. Forty years of problem-oriented policing: A review of progress in England and Wales. *Policing: A Journal of Policy and Practice*, 15(4): 2001–2014.

Burton, S. and McGregor, M. 2018. Enhancing SARA: A new approach in an increasingly complex world. *Crime Science*, 7(1): 1–5.

Callender, M., Cahalin, K., Cole, S.J., Hubbard, L. and Britton, I. 2020. Understanding the motivations, morale, and retention of special constables: Findings from a national survey. *Policing: A Journal of Policy and Practice*, 14(3): 670–685.

Calver, T. and Wainwright, D. 2018. How cuts changed council spending, in seven charts. *BBC News*, 5 December. Available at https://www.bbc.co.uk/news/uk-england-46443700 [Accessed 1 May 2019].

Cameron, D. 2011. PM's speech on Big Society. Available at https://www.gov.uk/government/speeches/pms-speech-on-big-society [Accessed 16 July 2019].

Carr, P.J. 2003. The new parochialism: The implications of the Beltway case for arguments concerning informal social control. *American Journal of Sociology* 108(6): 1249–1291.

Casey, L. 2008. *Engaging communities in fighting crime: A review by Louise Casey*. London: Cabinet Office. Available at http://news.bbc.co.uk/1/shared/bsp/hi/pdfs/18_06_08_caseyreport.pdf [Accessed 10 January 2014].

Charman, S. 2017. *Police socialisation, identity and culture: Becoming blue*. Cham: Palgrave Macmillan.

Christmas, H. and Srivastava, J. 2019. *Public health approaches in policing*. London: Public Health England, College of Policing.

Clark, T. and Taylor, M. 2014. Insecure Britain: Poll shines light on nation's economic anxiety. *The Guardian*. Available at https://www.theguardian.com/society/2014/jun/16/insecure-britain-poll-economic-recovery-immigration [Accessed 6 September 2023].

Clarke, R.V. and Hough, J.M. 1984. *Crime and police effectiveness* (Vol 81, No 1). London: HMSO.

Clarke, R.V. and Goldstein, H. 2002. Reducing theft at construction sites: Lessons from a problem-oriented project. University of Wisconsin Legal Studies Research Paper No. 1338. Available at https://ssrn.com/abstract=2540575

Clarke, R.V. and Eck, J.E. 2005. *Crime analysis for problem solvers in 60 small steps*. Washington, DC: US Department of Justice, Office of Community Oriented Policing Services.

Clarke, J., Newman, J., Smith, N., Vidler, E. and Westmarland, L. 2007. *Creating citizen-consumers: Changing publics and changing public services*. London: SAGE.

Cohen, L.E. and Felson, M. 1979. Social change and crime rate trends: A routine activity approach. *American Sociological Review*, 44(4): 588–608.

Coleman, J.S. 1988. Social capital in the creation of human capital. *American Journal of Sociology*, 94: S95–S120.

Colover, S. and Quinton, P. 2018. *Neighbourhood policing: Impact and implementation. Summary findings from a rapid evidence assessment*. Coventry: College of Policing. Available at http://whatworks.college.police.uk/Research/Pages/Published.aspx [Accessed 4 July 2018].

Constable, J. and Smith, J. 2015. Initial police training and the development of police occupational culture. In P. Wankhade and D. Weir (eds) *Police services: Leadership and management perspectives*. Cham: Springer, pp45–60.

Cooper, C., Anscombe, J., Avenell, J., McLean, F. and Morris, J. 2006. *A national evaluation of community support officers*. London: Home Office Research, Development and Statistics Directorate.

CoP (College of Policing). 2013. *Authorised professional practice: Engagement*. Available at https://www.college.police.uk/app/engagement-and-communication/engagement [Accessed 19 October 2022].

CoP (College of Policing). 2015a. *Estimating demand on the police service*. Coventry: College of Policing.

CoP (College of Policing). 2015b. *Delivering neighbourhood policing: A practice stocktake report of survey findings.* Coventry: College of Policing. Available at http://library.college.police.uk/docs/college-of-policing/NHP-Stockt ake-final-version-V1.pdf [Accessed 17 December 2017].

CoP (College of Policing). 2017b. *About us.* Available at https://www.coll ege.police.uk/About/Pages/default.aspx [Accessed 16 July 2019].

CoP (College of Policing). 2017c. *Policing Education Qualifications Framework (PEQF).* Available at https://www.college.police.uk/What-we-do/Learn ing/Policing-Education-Qualifications-Framework/Pages/Policing-Educat ion-Qualifications-Framework.aspx [Accessed 16 July 2019].

CoP (College of Policing). 2018a. *Modernising neighbourhood policing guidelines.* Coventry: College of Policing.

CoP (College of Policing). 2018b. *Neighbourhood policing guidelines: Supporting material for senior leaders.* Coventry: College of Policing.

CoP (College of Policing). 2018c. *Neighbourhood policing guidelines: Supporting material for frontline officers, staff and volunteers.* Coventry: College of Policing.

CoP (College of Policing). 2020. *Authorised professional practice: Communication.* Available at https://www.college.police.uk/app/engagement-and-communication/communication#digital-and-social-media [Accessed 15 November 2022].

CoP (College of Policing). 2022. *Crime reduction toolkit.* Available at https://www.college.police.uk/research/crime-reduction-toolkit [Accessed 12 December 2022].

Cordner, G. and Biebel, E.P. 2005. Problem-oriented policing in practice. *Criminology and Public Policy*, 4(2): 155–180.

Cosgrove, F. and Ramshaw, P. 2015. It is what you do as well as the way that you do it: The value and deployment of PCSOs in achieving public engagement. *Policing and Society*, 25(1): 77–96.

Crawford, A. 1999. *The local governance of crime: Appeals to community and partnerships.* Oxford: Clarendon Press.

Crawford, A. 2001. Joined-up but fragmented: Contradiction, ambiguity and ambivalence at the heart of New Labour's 'Third Way'. In R. Matthews and J. Pitts (eds) *Crime, Disorder and Community Safety: A New Agenda?* London: Routledge, pp54–80.

Crawford, A. 2006. 'Fixing broken promises?': Neighbourhood wardens and social capital. *Urban Studies* 43(5–6): 957–976.

Crawford, A. and Lister, S. 2004. The patchwork shape of reassurance policing in England and Wales: Integrated local security quilts or frayed, fragmented and fragile tangled webs? *Policing: An International Journal of Police Strategies and Management*, 27(3): 413–430.

Crawford, A. and Lister, S. 2006. Additional security patrols in residential areas: Notes from the marketplace. *Policing & Society*, 16(2): 164–188.

Crawford, A. and Evans, K. 2017. Crime prevention and community safety. In A. Liebling, S. Maruna and L. McAra (eds) *The Oxford handbook of criminology*. Oxford: Oxford University Press, pp797–824.

Crawford, A., Lister, S. and Wall, D. 2003. *Great expectations: Contracted community policing in New Earswick*. York: Joseph Rowntree Foundation.

Crawford, A., Lister, S. and Blackburn, S. 2005. *Plural policing: The mixed economy of visible patrols in England and Wales*. Bristol: Policy Press.

Dalgleish, D. and Myhill, A. 2004. *Reassuring the public: A review of international policing interventions*. London: Home Office Research, Development and Statistics Directorate.

Davies, A. and Thomas, R. 2008. Dixon of Dock Green got shot! Policing identity work and organizational change. *Public Administration*, 86(3): 627–642.

De Graaf, G. and Meijer, A. 2019. Social media and value conflicts: An explorative study of the Dutch police. *Public Administration Review*, 79(1): 82–92.

De Graaf, G., Huberts, L. and Smulders, R. 2016. Coping with public value conflicts. *Administration & Society*, 48(9): 1101–1127.

Deuchar, R., Miller, J. and Densley, J. 2019. The lived experience of stop and search in Scotland: There are two sides to every story. *Police Quarterly*, 22(4): 416–451.

Disney, R. and Simpson, P. 2017. *Police workforce and funding in England and Wales*. IFS Briefing Note BN208. London: Institute for Fiscal Studies. Available at https://www.ifs.org.uk/uploads/publications/bns/bn208.pdf [Accessed 26 June 2017].

Ditton, J., Bannister, J., Gilchrist, E. and Farrall, S. 1999. Afraid or angry? Recalibrating the 'fear' of crime. *International Review of Victimology*, 6(2): 83–99.

Downes, D. and Morgan, R. 1997. Dumping the 'hostages to fortune'? The politics of law and order in post-war Britain. In M. Maguire, R. Morgan and R. Reiner (eds) *The Oxford handbook of criminology*, 2nd edn. Oxford: Oxford University Press, pp87–134.

Eck, J.E. and Spelman, W. 1987. *Problem-solving: Problem-oriented policing in Newport News*. Washington, DC: U.S. Department of Justice, National Institute of Justice.

Eck, J.E. and Rosenbaum, D.P. 1994. The new police order: Effectiveness, equity and efficiency in community policing. In D.P. Rosenbaum (ed) *The challenge of community policing: Testing the promises*. Newbury Park: SAGE, pp3–26.

Elliott, R. and Nicholls, J. 1996. *It's good to talk: Lessons in public consultation and feedback*. London: Home Office Police Research Group.

Farrall, S. and Ditton, J. 1999. Improving the measurement of attitudinal responses: An example from a crime survey. *International Journal of Social Research Methodology*, 2(1): 55–68.

Fielding, N.G. 2005. Concepts and theory in community policing. *The Howard Journal of Criminal Justice*, 44(5): 460–472.

Finlayson, A. 1999. Third way theory. *The Political Quarterly*, 70(3): 271–279.

Flanagan, R. 2008. *The review of policing: Final report*. London: Home Office.

Fleming, J. and McLaughlin, E. 2012. Through a different lens: Researching the rise and fall of New Labour's 'public confidence agenda'. *Policing and Society*, 22(3): 280–294.

Forrest, S., Myhill, A. and Tilley, N. 2005. *Practical lessons for involving the community in crime and disorder problem-solving*. London: Home Office.

Foster, J. and Jones, C. 2010. 'Nice to do' and essential: Improving neighbourhood policing in an English police force. *Policing: A Journal of Policy and Practice*, 4(4): 395–402.

Furnham, A. 2000. The brainstorming myth. *Business Strategy Review*, 11(4): 21–28.

Gau, J.M. 2014. Unpacking collective efficacy: The relationship between social cohesion and informal social control. *Criminal Justice Studies*, 27(2): 210–225.

Giacomantonio, C., Bradford, B., Davies, M. and Martin, R. 2015. *Making and breaking barriers: Assessing the value of mounted police units in the UK*. Santa Monica and Cambridge: RAND Corporation.

Gill, C., Weisburd, D., Telep, C.W., Vitter, Z. and Bennett, T. 2014. Community-oriented policing to reduce crime, disorder and fear and increase satisfaction and legitimacy among citizens: A systematic review. *Journal of Experimental Criminology*, 10: 399–428.

Glynn, T.J. 1986. Neighborhood and sense of community. *Journal of Community Psychology*, 14(4): 341–352.

Goldsmith, A. 2015. Disgracebook policing: Social media and the rise of police indiscretion. *Policing and Society*, 25(3): 249–267.

Goldsmith, A. and McLaughlin, E. 2022. Policing's new vulnerability re-envisioning local accountability in an era of global outrage. *The British Journal of Criminology*, 62(3): 716–733.

Goldstein, H. 1979. Improving policing: A problem-oriented approach. *Crime and Delinquency*, 25(2): 236–258.

Goldstein, H. 1990. *Problem-oriented policing*. New York and London: McGraw-Hill.

Goldstein, H. 2018. On problem-oriented policing: The Stockholm lecture. *Crime Science*, 7(1): 1–9.

Goodman-Delahunty, J. 2010. Four ingredients: New recipes for procedural justice in Australian policing. *Policing: A Journal of Policy and Practice*, 4(4): 403–410.

Grace, S. 2020. Policing social distancing: Gaining and maintaining compliance in the age of coronavirus. *Policing: A Journal of Policy and Practice*, 14(4): 1034–1053.

Granovetter, M.S. 1973. The strength of weak ties. *American Journal of Sociology*, 78(6): 1360–1380.

Grimmelikhuijsen, S.G. and Meijer, A.J. 2015. Does Twitter increase perceived police legitimacy? *Public Administration Review*, 75(4): 598–607.

Grinc, R.M. 1994. 'Angels in marble': Problems in stimulating community involvement in community policing. *Crime and Delinquency*, 40(3): 437–468.

Hail, Y., Aston, L. and O'Neill, M. 2018. *Review of evidence: What effect do enforcement-orientated and engagement-orientated methods of visible policing have on public confidence?* Scottish Institute for Policing Research. Available at http://www.sipr.ac.uk/Plugin/Publications/assets/files/Review_methods_of_visible_policing_and_public_confidence_Hail_%20Aston_%20O'Neill.pdf [Accessed 11 May 2019].

Hand, C. 2022. Police stations closing at the rate of one per week, LBC reveals. *LBC*, 30 November. Available at https://www.lbc.co.uk/news/police-stations-closing-one-per-week-lbc-reveals/ [Accessed 30 November 2022].

Hardy, C., Lawrence, T.B. and Grant, D. 2005. Discourse and collaboration: The role of conversations and collective identity. *Academy of Management Review*, 30(1): 58–77.

Harfield, C.G. 1997. Consent, consensus or the management of dissent? Challenges to community consultation in a new policing environment. *Policing and Society*, 7(4): 271–289.

Harinam, V., Bavcevic, Z. and Ariel, B. 2022. Spatial distribution and developmental trajectories of crime versus crime severity: Do not abandon the count-based model just yet. *Crime Science*, 11(1): 1–15.

Harkin, D. 2014. 'Civilizing policing'? What can police-public consultation forums achieve for police reform, 'democratic policing' and police legitimacy? PhD thesis, University of Edinburgh. Available at https://www.era.lib.ed.ac.uk/handle/1842/14178 [Accessed 5 June 2016].

Harkin, D. 2015. Simmel, the police form and the limits of democratic policing. *British Journal of Criminology*, 55(4): 730–746.

Harkin, D. 2018. Community safety partnerships: The limits and possibilities of 'policing with the community'. *Crime Prevention and Community Safety*, 20(2): 125–136.

Hawdon, J. 2008. Legitimacy, trust, social capital and policing styles: A theoretical statement. *Police Quarterly*, 11(2): 182–201.

Herbert, S. 2006. Tangled up in blue: Conflicting paths to police legitimacy. *Theoretical Criminology*, 10(4): 481–504.

Higgins, A. 2017. *Neighbourhood policing: A police force typology*. London: The Police Foundation. Available at http://www.police-foundation.org.uk/publication/neighbourhood-policing-a-police-force-typology/ [Accessed 10 May 2017].

Higgins, A. 2018. *The future of neighbourhood policing*. London: The Police Foundation. Available at http://www.police-foundation.org.uk/publication/future-neighbourhood-policing/ [Accessed 30 May 2019].

Higgins, A. and Hales, G. 2017. *Police effectiveness in a changing world paper 4: A natural experiment in neighbourhood policing*. London: The Police Foundation. Available at http://www.police-foundation.org.uk/2017/wp-content/uploads/2017/06/changing_world_paper_4.pdf [Accessed 15 February 2017].

Hipp, J.R. 2016. Collective efficacy: How is it conceptualized, how is it measured and does it really matter for understanding perceived neighborhood crime and disorder? *Journal of Criminal Justice*, 46: 32–44.

Hipp, J.R. and Kim, Y.A. 2017. Measuring crime concentration across cities of varying sizes: Complications based on the spatial and temporal scale employed. *Journal of Quantitative Criminology*, 33(3): 595–632.

HMIC (Her Majesty's Inspectorate of Constabulary). 2008. *Serving neighbourhoods and individuals: A thematic report on neighbourhood policing and developing citizen focus policing*. London: HMIC. Available at https://www.justiceinspectorates.gov.uk/hmicfrs/media/serving-neighbourhoods-and-individuals-20081031.pdf [Accessed 25 May 2019].

HMIC (Her Majesty's Inspectorate of Constabulary). 2010. *Anti-social behaviour: Stop the rot*. London: HMIC.

HMIC (Her Majesty's Inspectorate of Constabulary). 2013. *Policing in austerity: Rising to the challenge*. London: HMIC.

HMIC (Her Majesty's Inspectorate of Constabulary). 2017. *PEEL: Police effectiveness 2016. A national overview*. London: HMIC.

HMICFRS (Her Majesty's Inspectorate of Constabulary and Fire and Rescue Services). 2020. *A call for help: Police contact management through call handling and control rooms in 2018/19*. Available at https://www.justiceinspectorates.gov.uk/hmicfrs/wp-content/uploads/a-call-for-help-police-contact-management-call-handling-control-rooms-2018-19.pdf [Accessed 19 August 2022].

HMICFRS (Her Majesty's Inspectorate of Constabulary and Fire and Rescue Services). 2021a. *Policing in the pandemic: The police response to the coronavirus pandemic during 2020*. Available at https://www.justiceinspectorates.gov.uk/hmicfrs/publication-html/the-police-response-to-the-coronavirus-pandemic-during-2020/ [Accessed 1 December 2022].

HMICFRS (Her Majesty's Inspectorate of Constabulary and Fire and Rescue Services). 2021b. *The Sarah Everard vigil: An inspection of the Metropolitan Police Service's policing of a vigil held in commemoration of Sarah Everard on Clapham Common on Saturday 13 March 2021*. Available at https://www.justiceinspectorates.gov.uk/hmicfrs/wp-content/uploads/inspection-of-mps-policing-vigil-commemoration-sarah-everard-clapham-common.pdf/ [Accessed 1 December 2022].

HMICFRS (Her Majesty's Inspectorate of Constabulary and Fire & Rescue Services). 2022. *State of policing: The annual assessment of Policing in England and Wales 2021*. London: Her Majesty's Chief Inspector of Constabulary and Fire & Rescue Services. Available at: https://www.justiceinspectora tes.gov.uk/hmicfrs/wp-content/uploads/State-of- policing-2021-1-single-page.pdf [Accessed 5 September 2023].

HMICS (Her Majesty's Inspectorate of Constabulary for Scotland). 2002. *Narrowing the gap: Police visibility and public reassurance*. Edinburgh: The Stationery Office.

Hohl, K., Bradford, B. and Stanko, E.A. 2010. Influencing trust and confidence in the London Metropolitan Police: Results from an experiment testing the effect of leaflet drops on public opinion. *British Journal of Criminology*, 50(3): 491–513.

Holdaway, S. 1977. Changes in urban policing. *British Journal of Sociology*, 28(2): 119–137.

Home Office. 2003. *Building safer communities together*. London: HMSO.

Home Office. 2004a. *Building communities, beating crime*. London: HMSO.

Home Office. 2004b. *Confident communities in a secure Britain: The Home Office strategic plan 2004–08*. London: HMSO.

Home Office. 2006. *Neighbourhood policing progress report May 2006*. London: HMSO.

Home Office. 2009. *Protecting the public: Supporting the police to succeed*. London: HMSO.

Home Office. 2010a. *Policing in the 21st century: Reconnecting police and the people*. London: Home Office.

Home Office. 2010b. *Safe and confident neighbourhoods strategy: Next steps in neighbourhood policing*. London: Home Office.

Home Office. 2021. *Beating crime plan*. Available at https://www.gov.uk/gov ernment/publications/beating-crime-plan/beating-crime-plan [Accessed 13 July 2022].

Hope, T. 2005. The new local governance of community safety in England and Wales. *Canadian Journal of Criminology and Criminal Justice*, 47(2): 369–388.

Hough, M. 2017. The discovery of fear of crime in the UK. In M. Lee and G. Mythen (eds) *The Routledge international handbook on fear of crime*. New York: Routledge, pp35–46.

Hough, M. and Tilley, N. 1998. *Auditing crime and disorder: Guidance for local partnerships*. London: Home Office, Police Research Group.

House of Commons Home Affairs Committee. 2018. *Policing for the future. Tenth Report of Session 2017–19. Report, together with formal minutes relating to the report*. London: HMSO.

Hughes, G. and Gilling, D. 2004. 'Mission impossible'? The habitus of the community safety manager and the new expertise in the local partnership governance of crime and safety. *Criminal Justice*, 4: 129–149.

Hughes, G. and Rowe, M. 2007. Neighbourhood policing and community safety: Researching the instabilities of the local governance of crime, disorder and security in contemporary UK. *Criminology and Criminal Justice*, 7(4): 317–346.

The Independent. 2010. Police cuts need not affect front line, says Theresa May. *The Independent*, 18 November. Available at https://www.independent. co.uk/news/uk/politics/police-cuts-need-not-affect-front-line-says-ther esa-may-2137551.html [Accessed 16 July 2019].

Innes, M. 2004. Reinventing tradition? Reassurance, neighbourhood security and policing. *Criminal Justice*, 4(2): 151–171.

Innes, M. 2005a. Why 'soft' policing is hard: On the curious development of reassurance policing, how it became neighbourhood policing and what this signifies about the politics of police reform. *Journal of Community and Applied Social Psychology*, 15(3): 156–169.

Innes, M. 2005b. What's your problem? Signal crimes and citizen-focused problem solving. *Criminology and Public Policy*, 4(2): 187–200.

Innes, M. 2007. The reassurance function. *Policing: A Journal of Policy and Practice*, 1(2): 132–141.

Innes, M. and Fielding, N. 2002. From community to communicative policing: 'Signal crimes' and the problem of public reassurance. *Sociological Research Online*, 7(2): 1–12.

Innes, M. and Roberts, C. 2008. Reassurance policing, community intelligence and the co-production of neighbourhood order. In T. Williamson (ed) *The handbook of knowledge-based policing: Current conceptions and future directions*. London: Wiley and Sons, pp241–262.

Innes, M. and Weston, N. 2010. *Re-thinking the policing of anti-social behaviour*. London: HMIC.

Innes, M., Roberts, C., Innes, H. and Lowe, T. 2020. *Neighbourhood policing: The rise and fall of a policing model*. Oxford: Oxford University Press.

Irving, B. 1986. *Independent evaluation of an experiment in neighbourhood policing in Notting Hill*. London: Police Foundation.

Irving, B., Bird, C., Hibberd, M. and Willmore, J. 1989. *Neighbourhood policing: The natural history of a policing experiment*. London: Police Foundation.

Jack, K., Frondigoun, L. and Smith, R. 2021. Implementing an asset-based approach: A case study of innovative community policing from Hawkhill, Scotland. *The Police Journal*, 94(3): 353–371.

Jackson, J. and Sunshine, J. 2007. Public confidence in policing. *The British Journal of Criminology*, 47(2): 214–233.

Jackson, J. and Bradford, B. 2009. Crime, policing and social order: On the expressive nature of public confidence in policing. *The British Journal of Sociology*, 60(3): 493–521.

Jackson, J. and Bradford, B. 2010. What is trust and confidence in the police? *Policing: A Journal of Policy and Practice*, 4(3): 241–248.

Jacques, P. 2022. Humberside Police congratulated for 'outstanding' performance. 25 November. Available at https://www.policeprofessional. com/news/humberside-police-congratulated-for-outstanding-performance/ [Accessed 10 December 2022].

Jessop, B. 2000. The dynamics of partnership and governance failure: The new politics of local governance in Britain. In G. Stoker (ed) *The new politics of local governance in Britain*. Basingstoke: Macmillan, pp11–32.

Johnston, L. 2003. From 'pluralisation' to 'the police extended family': Discourses on the governance of community policing in Britain. *International Journal of the Sociology of Law*, 31(3): 185–204.

Johnston, L. 2007. 'Keeping the family together': Police Community Support Officers and the 'police extended family' in London. *Policing & Society*, 17(2): 119–140.

Jones, T. and Newburn, T. 2001. *Widening access: Improving police relations with hard to reach groups*. London: Home Office, Policing and Reducing Crime Unit.

Kelling, G.L., Pate, T., Dieckman, D. and Brown, C. 1974. *The Kansas City preventive patrol experiment: A technical report*. Washington, DC: Police Foundation.

Kleinhans, R. and Bolt, G. 2014. More than just fear: On the intricate interplay between perceived neighborhood disorder, collective efficacy, and action. *Journal of Urban Affairs*, 36(3): 420–446.

Kochel, T.R. and Weisburd, D. 2017. Assessing community consequences of implementing hot spots policing in residential areas: Findings from a randomized field trial. *Journal of Experimental Criminology*, 13(2): 143–170.

Kretzmann, J. and McKnight, J. 1993. *Building communities from the inside out: A path toward finding and mobilizing a community's assets*. Chicago: The Asset-Based Community Development Institute.

Labour Party. 2022. *Britain in 2030: Stronger together for safe and secure communities*. Available at https://labour.org.uk/stronger-together/britain-2030/safe-communities/ [Accessed 9 November 2022].

Leigh, A., Read, T., Tilley, N. and Webb, B. 1996. *Problem-oriented policing: Brit pop*. London: Home Office Police Research Group.

Lentz, S.A. and Chaires, R.H. 2007. The invention of Peel's principles: A study of policing 'textbook' history. *Journal of Criminal Justice*, 35(1): 69–79.

Lewis, P., Newburn, T., Taylor, M., Mcgillivray, C., Greenhill, A., Frayman, H. and Proctor, R. 2011. *Reading the riots: Investigating England's summer of disorder*. London: The London School of Economics and Political Science and the Guardian.

Lind, E.A. and Tyler, T.R. 1988. *The social psychology of procedural justice.* New York and London: Plenum Press.

Lipsky, M. 1980. *Street-level bureaucracy: Dilemmas of the individual in public services.* New York: Russell Sage Foundation.

Lister, S. 2014. Scrutinising the role of the Police and Crime Panel in the new era of police governance in England and Wales. *Safer Communities,* 13(1): 22–31.

Lister, S. and Rowe, M. 2015. Electing police and crime commissioners in England and Wales: Prospecting for the democratisation of policing. *Policing and Society,* 25(4): 358–377.

Lister, S., Adams, B. and Phillips, S. 2015. *Evaluation of police-community engagement practices: An exploratory knowledge platform for policing: Exploiting knowledge assets, utilising data and piloting research co-production.* University of Leeds. Available at http://www.law.leeds.ac.uk/research/projects/an-exploratory-knowledge-platform-for-policing/ [Accessed 30 August 2017].

Loader, I. 1997. Policing and the social: Questions of symbolic power. *British Journal of Sociology,* 48(1): 1–18.

Loader, I. 2000. Plural policing and democratic governance. *Social and Legal Studies,* 9(3): 323–345.

Loader, I. 2006. Policing, recognition, and belonging. *The Annals of the American Academy of Political and Social Science,* 605(1): 201–221.

Loader, I. 2020. *Revisiting the police mission: Strategic review of policing in England and Wales.* London: The Police Foundation.

Loader, I. and Sparks, R. 2012. Beyond lamentation: Towards a democratic egalitarian politics of crime and justice. In T. Newburn and J. Peay (eds) *Policing: Politics, culture and control.* London: Hart, pp11–41.

Loftus, B. 2009. *Police culture in a changing world.* Oxford: Oxford University Press.

Lombardo, R.M., Olson, D. and Staton, M. 2010. The Chicago alternative policing strategy: A reassessment of the CAPS program. *Policing: An International Journal of Police Strategies and Management,* 33(4): 586–606.

Longstaff, A., Willer, J., Chapman, J., Czarnomski, S. and Graham, J. 2015. *Neighbourhood policing: Past, present and future.* London: The Police Foundation.

Loveday, B. and Smith, R. 2015. A critical evaluation of current and future roles of police community support officers and neighbourhood wardens within the Metropolitan Police Service and London boroughs: Utilising 'low-cost high-value' support services in a period of financial austerity. *International Journal of Police Science and Management,* 17(2): 74–80.

Mackenzie, S. and Henry, A. 2009. *Community policing: A review of the evidence.* Edinburgh: Scottish Government Social Research.

Manning, P.K. 1997. *Police work: the social organisation of policing,* 2nd edn. Prospect Heights: Waveland Press Inc.

Marenin, O. 1998. The goal of democracy in international police assistance programs. *Policing: An International Journal of Police Strategies and Management*, 21(1): 159–177.

Mastrofski, S.D. 2006. Community policing: A skeptical view. In D. Weisburd and A.A. Braga (eds) *Police innovation: Contrasting perspectives*. Cambridge: Cambridge University Press, pp44–73.

Mathie, A. and Cunningham, G. 2003. From clients to citizens: Asset-based community development as a strategy for community-driven development. *Development in Practice*, 13(5): 474–486.

May, T. 2011. Speech to the Conservative Party Conference. 4 October. Available at https://www.politics.co.uk/comment-analysis/2011/10/04/theresa-may-speech-in-full [Accessed 14 March 2015]

May, T. 2015. Home Secretary at the Police Reform Summit. Speech. 8 December. Available at https://www.gov.uk/government/speeches/home-secretary-at-the-police-reform-summit [Accessed 16 July 2019].

McCarthy, D. and O'Neill, M. 2014. The police and partnership working: Reflections on recent research. *Policing: A Journal of Policy and Practice*, 8(3): 243–253.

McLaughlin, E. 2005. Forcing the issue: New Labour, new localism and the democratic renewal of police accountability. *The Howard Journal of Criminal Justice*, 44(5): 473–489.

McLaughlin, E. 2008. 'Last one out, turn off the "blue lamp"': The geographical 'placing' of police performance management. *Policing: A Journal of Policy and Practice*, 2(3): 266–275.

McLaughlin, E. and Murji, K. 1998. Resistance through representation: 'Storylines', advertising and police federation campaigns. *Policing and Society*, 8(4): 367–399.

Millie, A. 2012. Police stations, architecture and public reassurance. *British Journal of Criminology*, 52(6): 1092–1112.

Millie, A. 2013. The policing task and the expansion (and contraction) of British policing. *Criminology and Criminal Justice*, 13(2): 143–160.

Millie, A. and Bullock, K. 2012. Re-imagining policing post-austerity. *British Academy Review*, 19: 16–18.

Morgan, R. and Maggs, C. 1985. *Setting the P.A.C.E. police community consultation arrangements in England and Wales*. Bath: Centre for the Analysis of Social Policy, University of Bath.

Morgan, R. and Newburn, T. 1997. *The future of policing*. Oxford: Clarendon Press.

Murphy, C. and Muir, G. 1985. *Community-based policing: A review of the critical issues*. Ottawa: Solicitor General of Canada.

Mutongwizo, T., Holley, C., Shearing, C.D. and Simpson, N.P. 2021. Resilience policing: An emerging response to shifting harm landscapes and reshaping community policing. *Policing: A Journal of Policy and Practice*, 15(1): 606–621.

Myhill, A. 2006. *Community engagement in policing: Lessons from the literature.* London: Home Office.

Myhill, A. and Beak, K. 2008. *Public confidence in the police.* London: National Police Improvement Agency (NPIA).

Myhill, A., Dalgleish, D., Docking, M., Myhill, A. and Yarrow, S. 2003. *The role of police authorities in public engagement.* London: Home Office.

NCIS (National Criminal Intelligence Service). 2000. *The national intelligence model.* London: NCIS.

Newman, J. 2001. Joined-up government: The politics of partnership. In L. Budd, J. Charlesworth and R. Paton (eds) *Making policy happen.* London: Routledge, pp194–200.

Nilsson, M. and Jonsson, C. 2023. Building relational peace: Police-community relations in post-accord Colombia. *Policing and Society*, 33(5): 518–536.

Nisbet, R. 1953. *The quest for community.* New York: Orford.

NPCC (National Police Chiefs' Council). 2017. *Better understanding demand: Policing the future.* London: NPCC Performance Management Coordination Committee

NPIA (National Policing Improvement Agency). 2010. *Local policing and confidence.* London: NPIA.

Ofcom (Office of Communications). 2018. *Adults' media use and attitudes report 2018.* London: Ofcom.

O'Malley, L. and Grace, S. 2021. Social capital and co-location: A case study of policing anti-social behaviour. *International Journal of Police Science and Management*, 23(3): 306–316.

O'Neill, M. 2015. The case for the acceptable 'other': The impact of partnerships, PCSOs and neighbourhood policing on diversity in policing. *Policing: A Journal of Policy and Practice*, 9(1): 77–88.

ONS (Office for National Statistics). 2021. *Confidence in the local police.* Available at https://www.ethnicity-facts-figures.service.gov.uk/crime-just ice-and-the-law/policing/confidence-in-the-local-police/latest [Accessed 6 September 2023].

O'Reilly, C. 2020. Neighbourhood policing: Community, confidence and legitimacy in a London borough. PhD thesis, Anglia Ruskin University. Available at https://arro.anglia.ac.uk/id/eprint/706855/ [Accessed 19 December 2022].

O'Reilly, C. 2021. Key issues in contemporary policing: Models of police and policing. *Policing Insight*, 13 April. Available at https://policinginsight. com/features/key-issues-in-contemporary-policing-models-police-polic ing/ [Accessed 17 December 2022].

O'Reilly, C. 2023. Doing the right thing? Value conflicts and community policing. *Policing and Society*, 33(1): 1–17.

O'Reilly, C., Agnew-Pauley, W. and Lundrigan, S. 2022. Restoring public confidence through the delivery of improved community policing in Rackhamshire. *Safer Communities*, 21(2): 69–84.

PA Consulting Group. 2001. *Diary of a police officer.* Police Research Series Paper 149. London: Home Office.

Paskell, C. 2007. 'Plastic police' or 'community support'? The role of Police Community Support Officers within low-income neighbourhoods. *European Urban and Regional Studies*, 14(4): 349–361.

Pate, A.M., Wycoff, M.A., Skogan, W.G. and Sherman, L.W. 1986. *Reducing fear of crime in Houston and Newark.* Washington, DC: Police Foundation.

Peaslee, L. 2009. Community policing and social service partnerships: Lessons from New England. *Police Practice and Research*, 10(2): 115–131.

Pepper, I. 2014. Do part-time volunteer police officers aspire to be regular police officers? *The Police Journal*, 87(2): 105–113.

Perkins, M. 2016. Modelling public confidence of the police: How perceptions of the police differ between neighborhoods in a city. *Police Practice and Research*, 17(2): 113–125.

Pickles, E. 2010. *Eric Pickles 'shows us the money'.* Ministry of Housing, Communities and Local Government, 12 August. Available at https://www.gov.uk/government/news/eric-pickles-shows-us-the-money-as-depar tmental-books-are-opened-to-an-army-of-armchair-auditors [Accessed 11 December 2022].

Police Federation of England and Wales and Police Superintendents' Association. 1990. *Operational policing review 1990.* Surbiton: Police Federation Joint Consultative Committee.

Police Foundation. 2022. *A new mode of protection: Final report of the strategic review of policing in England and Wales.* London: Police Foundation.

Povey, K. 2001. *Open all hours: A thematic inspection report on the role of police visibility and accessibility in public reassurance.* London: HMIC.

Putnam, R.D. 1995a. Bowling alone: America's declining social capital. *Journal of Democracy*, 6(1): 65–78.

Putnam, R.D. 1995b. Tuning in, tuning out: The strange disappearance of social capital in America. *Political Science and Politics*, 28(4): 664–683.

Quinton, P. 2011. *The impact of information about crime and policing on public perceptions: The results of a randomised controlled trial.* London: NPIA.

Quinton, P. and Tuffin, R. 2007. Neighbourhood change: The impact of the national reassurance policing programme. *Policing: A Journal of Policy and Practice*, 1(2): 149–160.

Quinton, P. and Morris, J. 2008. *Neighbourhood policing: The impact of piloting and early national implementation.* London: Home Office.

Radburn, M. and Stott, C. 2019. The social psychological processes of 'procedural justice': Concepts, critiques and opportunities. *Criminology and Criminal Justice*, 19(4): 421–438.

Ratcliffe, J.H. 2018. *Reducing crime: A companion for police leaders*. Abingdon and New York: Routledge.

Ralph, L. 2022. The dynamic nature of police legitimacy on social media. *Policing and Society*, 32(7): 817–831.

Ralph, L., Jones, M., Rowe, M. and Millie, A. 2022. Maintaining police-citizen relations on social media during the COVID-19 pandemic. *Policing and Society*, 32(6): 764–777.

Read, T. and Tilley, N. 2000. *Not rocket science? Problem-solving and crime reduction*. London: Home Office.

Reiner, R. 2009. Consent. In A. Wakefield and J. Fleming (eds) *The SAGE dictionary of policing*. London: SAGE, pp52–54.

Reiner, R. 2010. *The politics of the police*. Oxford: Oxford University Press.

Reiner, R. 2013. Who governs? Democracy, plutocracy, science and prophecy in policing. *Criminology and Criminal Justice*, 13(2): 161–180.

Rhodes, R.A.W. 1997. *Understanding governance: Policy networks, governance, reflexivity and accountability*. Buckingham: Open University Press.

Rix, A., Joshua, F., Maguire, M. and Morton, S. 2009. *Improving public confidence in the police: A review of the evidence*. London: Home Office Research, Development and Statistics Directorate.

Robinson, A. 2006. *Police community support officers: A literature and policy review*. Sheffield: Hallam Centre for Community Justice.

Rogers, B. and Houston, T. 2004. *Re-inventing the police station: Police-public relations, reassurance and the future of the police estate*. London: IPPR.

Rogers, C. 2016. *Plural policing: Theory and practice*. Bristol: Policy Press.

Roth, J.A., Ryan, J., Gaffigan, S., Koper, C., Moore, M., Roehl, J. et al. 2000. *National evaluation of the COPS program: Title I of the 1994 Crime Act*. US Washington, DC: U.S. Department of Justice, National Institute of Justice.

Salisbury, H. 2004. *Public attitudes to the criminal justice system: The impact of providing information to British Crime Survey respondents*. London: Home Office.

Salmi, S., Voeten, M.J. and Keskinen, E. 2000. Relation between police image and police visibility. *Journal of Community and Applied Social Psychology*, 10(6): 433–447.

Sampson, R.J. 2002. Transcending tradition: New directions in community research, Chicago style. *Criminology*, 40(2): 213–230.

Savage, S.P. 2007a. *Police reform: Forces for change*. Oxford: Oxford University Press.

Savage, S.P. 2007b. Neighbourhood policing and the reinvention of the constable. *Policing: A Journal of Policy and Practice*, 1(2): 203–213.

Scarman, L.G. 1982. *The Scarman report: The Brixton disorders, 10–12 April 1981*. Harmondsworth: Penguin Books.

Scott, J.D. 2002. Assessing the relationship between police-community coproduction and neighborhood-level social capital. *Journal of Contemporary Criminal Justice*, 18(2): 147–166.

Sheldon, D. 2021. Policing the pandemic: Maintaining compliance and legitimacy during Covid-19. *King's Law Journal*, 32(1): 14–25.

Sherman, L.W. 2013. The rise of evidence-based policing: Targeting, testing, and tracking. *Crime and Justice*, 42(1): 377–451.

Sherman, L.W. and Weisburd, D. 1995. General deterrent effects of police patrol in crime 'hot spots': A randomized, controlled trial. *Justice Quarterly*, 12(4): 625–648.

Sherman, L.W. and Eck, J.E. 2003. Policing for crime prevention. In D. Farrington, D. Layton MacKenzie, L.W. Sherman and B.C. Welsh (eds) *Evidence-based crime prevention*. London: Routledge, pp309–343.

Sherman, L.W., Gartin, P.R. and Buerger, M.E. 1989. Hot spots of predatory crime: Routine activities and the criminology of place. *Criminology*, 27(1): 27–56.

Sherman, L.W., Neyroud, P.W. and Neyroud, E. 2016. The Cambridge crime harm index: Measuring total harm from crime based on sentencing guidelines. *Policing: A Journal of Policy and Practice*, 10(3): 171–183.

Sidebottom, A. and Tilley, N. 2011. Improving problem-oriented policing: The need for a new model? *Crime Prevention and Community Safety*, 13(2): 79–101.

Sidebottom, A., Bullock, K., Armitage, R., Ashby, M., Clemmow, C., Kirby, S., Laycock, G. and Tilley, N. 2020. *Problem-oriented policing in England and Wales 2019*. Coventry: College of Policing.

Silver, E. and Miller, L.L. 2004. Sources of informal social control in Chicago neighborhoods. *Criminology*, 42(3): 551–584.

Simmel, G. 2009. *Sociology: Inquiries into the construction of social forms*. Leiden and Boston: Brill.

Simpson, R. 2017. The Police Officer Perception Project (POPP): An experimental evaluation of factors that impact perceptions of the police. *Journal of Experimental Criminology*, 13(3): 393–415.

Sindall, K. and Sturgis, P. 2013. Austerity policing: Is visibility more important than absolute numbers in determining public confidence in the police? *European Journal of Criminology*, 10(2): 137–153.

Singer, L. 2004. *Reassurance policing: An evaluation of the local management of community safety*. London: Home Office Research, Development and Statistics Directorate.

Singer, L. and Cooper, S. 2009. Improving public confidence in the criminal justice system: An evaluation of a communication activity. *The Howard Journal of Criminal Justice*, 48(5): 485–500.

Skogan, W.G. 2006. Asymmetry in the impact of encounters with police. *Policing & Society*, 16(2): 99–126.

Skogan, W.G. 2008. An overview of community policing: Origins, concepts and implementation. In T. Williamson (ed) *The handbook of knowledge based policing: Current conceptions and future directions*. Chichester: John Wiley and Sons, pp43–58.

Skogan, W.G. and Hartnett, S.M. 1997. *Community policing, Chicago style*. New York and Oxford: Oxford University Press.

Skogan, W.G. and Steiner, L. 2004. *CAPS at ten: Community policing in Chicago. An evaluation of Chicago's alternative policing strategy*. Chicago: Institute for Policy Research, Northwestern University.

Skogan, W.G., Hartnett, S.M., Comey, J.T., Dubois, J. and Kaiser, M. 1999. *On the beat: Police and community problem solving*. Boulder: Westview Press. Available at http://citeseerx.ist.psu.edu/viewdoc/download?doi= 10.1.1.685.8354andrep=rep1andtype=pdf [Accessed 25 May 2019].

Smith, R. and Somerville, P. 2013. The long goodbye: A note on the closure of rural police-stations and the decline of rural policing in Britain. *Policing: A Journal of Policy and Practice*, 7(4): 348–358.

Sorg, E.T., Haberman, C.P., Ratcliffe, J.H. and Groff, E.R. 2013. Foot patrol in violent crime hot spots: The longitudinal impact of deterrence and posttreatment effects of displacement. *Criminology*, 51(1): 65–101.

Spelman, W. 1995. Criminal careers of public places. *Crime and Place*, 4: 115–144.

Stanko, E.A. and Dawson, P. 2016. *Police use of research evidence: Recommendations for improvement*. Cham: Springer International Publishing.

Stanley, L. 2016. Legitimacy gaps, taxpayer conflict and the politics of austerity in the UK. *The British Journal of Politics and International Relations*, 18(2): 389–406.

Stevens, J. 2013. *Policing for a better Britain: Report of the independent police commission*. London: Independent Police Commission.

Stewart, J. 2009. *Public policy values*. London: Palgrave Macmillan.

Stott, C., Radburn, M., Pearson, G., Kyprianides, A., Harrison, M. and Rowlands, D. 2022. Police powers and public assemblies: Learning from the Clapham Common 'vigil' during the Covid-19 pandemic. *Policing: A Journal of Policy and Practice*, 16(1): 73–94.

Sutherland, J. 2014. *The PCSO review: An evaluation of the role, value and establishment of police community support officers within Cambridgeshire Constabulary*. Huntingdon: Cambridgeshire Constabulary.

Szczepaniak, A. 2007. The place of the Royal Canadian Mounted Police in the perception of Canada as a 'safe place'. In C. Bates, G. Huggan, M. Marinkova and J. Orr (eds) *Visions of Canada – visions du Canada*. Brno: Central European Association for Canadian Studies, pp35–49.

Szreter, S. 2002. The state of social capital: Bringing back in power, politics and history. *Theory and Society*, 31(5): 573–621.

Szreter, S. and Woolcock, M. 2004. Health by association? Social capital, social theory and the political economy of public health. *International Journal of Epidemiology*, 33(4): 650–667.

Telep, C.W. and Weisburd, D. 2012. What is known about the effectiveness of police practices in reducing crime and disorder? *Police Quarterly*, 15(4): 331–357.

Terpstra, J. and Fyfe, N.R. 2015. Mind the implementation gap? Police reform and local policing in the Netherlands and Scotland. *Criminology & Criminal Justice*, 15(5): 527–544.

Terpstra, J., Fyfe, N.R. and Salet, R. 2019. The abstract police: A conceptual exploration of unintended changes of police organisations. *The Police Journal*, 92(4): 339–359.

Thacher, D. and Rein, M. 2004. Managing value conflict in public policy. *Governance*, 17(4): 457–486.

Tilley, N. 2008. The development of community policing in England: Networks, knowledge and neighbourhoods. In T. Williamson (ed) *The handbook of knowledge based policing: Current conceptions and future directions*. Chichester: John Wiley and Sons Ltd, pp95–116.

Tilley, N. 2010. Whither problem-oriented policing. *Criminology and Public Policy*, 9(1): 183–195.

Tilley, N. and Scott, M.S. 2012. The past, present and future of POP. *Policing: A Journal of Policy and Practice*, 6(2): 122–132.

Tobitt, C. 2021. Survey shows people more likely to trust local news produced on patch – and willing to pay average of £1.30 per month. *Press Gazette*, 30 September. Available at https://pressgazette.co.uk/news/survey-people-more-likely-to-trust-local-news-produced-on-patch-pay-average-of-1-30-month/ [Accessed 3 December 2022].

Tuffin, R., Morris, J. and Poole, A. 2006. *An evaluation of the impact of the National Reassurance Policing Programme* (Vol 296). London: Home Office Research, Development and Statistics Directorate.

Turley, C., Ranns, H., Callanan, M., Blackwell, A. and Newburn, T. 2012. *Delivering neighbourhood policing in partnership*. London: Home Office.

Tyler, T.R. 2004. Enhancing police legitimacy. *Annals of the American Academy of Political and Social Science*, 593: 84–99.

Tyler, T.R. 2006. *Why people obey the law*. Princeton and Oxford: Princeton University Press.

Tyler, T.R. and Fagan, J. 2008. Legitimacy and cooperation: Why do people help the police fight crime in their communities? *Ohio State Journal of Criminology*, 6(231): 231–275.

Uchida, C.D. 1993. The development of the American police: An historical overview. *Critical Issues in Policing: Contemporary Readings*, 3: 19–35.

Ungoed-Thomas, J., Harper, T. and Shveda, K. 2018. 600 police stations shut in eight years. *The Sunday Times*, 2 September. Available at https://www.thetimes.co.uk/article/600-police-stations-shut-in-eight-years-nvjdjwmwj [Accessed 16 June 2019].

Vidler, E. and Clarke, J. 2005. Creating citizen-consumers: New Labour and the remaking of public services. *Public Policy and Administration*, 20(2): 19–37.

Waddington, P.A. 1999. Police (canteen) sub-culture: An appreciation. *The British Journal of Criminology*, 39(2): 287–309.

Wakefield, A. 2006. *The value of foot patrol: A review of research*. London: Police Foundation.

Wakefield, A. 2007. Continuing the discussion on community policing, issue 2 carry on constable? Revaluing foot patrol. *Policing: A Journal of Policy and Practice*, 1(3): 342–355.

Wallace, A. 2010. New neighbourhoods, new citizens? Challenging 'community' as a framework for social and moral regeneration under New Labour in the UK. *International Journal of Urban and Regional Research*, 34(4): 805–819.

Walsh, J.P. and O'Connor, C. 2019. Social media and policing: A review of recent research. *Sociology Compass*, 13(1): 1–14. https://doi.org/10.1111/soc4.12648

Walzer, M. 1994. *Thick and thin: Moral argument at home and abroad*. Notre Dame, IN: University of Notre Dame Press.

Weisburd, D. 2018. Hot spots of crime and place-based prevention. *Criminology and Public Policy*, 17(1): 5–25.

Wilson, H. 1963. *Labour's plan for science*. London: Labour Party.

Wilson, J.Q. and Kelling, G.L. 1982. Broken windows. *Atlantic Monthly*, 249(3): 29–38.

Wood, J., Sorg, E.T., Groff, E.R., Ratcliffe, J.H. and Taylor, C.J. 2014. Cops as treatment providers: Realities and ironies of police work in a foot patrol experiment. *Policing and Society*, 24(3): 362–379.

Wood, M.A. and McGovern, A. 2021. Memetic copaganda: Understanding the humorous turn in police image work. *Crime, Media, Culture*, 17(3): 305–326.

Wünsch, D. and Hohl, K. 2009. Evidencing a 'good practice model' of police communication: The impact of local policing newsletters on public confidence. *Policing: A Journal of Policy and Practice*, 3(4): 331–339.

Zhao, J.S., Schneider, M. and Thurman, Q. 2002. The effect of police presence on public fear reduction and satisfaction: A review of the literature. *The Justice Professional*, 15(3): 273–299.

Index